D1170750

100 Masterpieces of
Australian Painting

Introduced by William Splatt

100 Masterpieces of Australian Painting

Notes on the artists by Barbara Burton
Commentaries on the plates by William Splatt

Rigby

Introduction

Australia has been settled by Europeans for nearly two hundred years. Before this there was nothing that Western eyes would have called art, although today a more enlightened opinion eagerly seeks out genuine aboriginal artefacts. None of these, however, has influenced the painting of Europeans or their descendants to any great extent; Australian art as we know it is of purely European origin. It falls naturally into three parts.

There are those paintings made by Europeans for other Europeans; made by painters who were never quite at home in the strange new land. They wished to show this strangeness to those who would otherwise never see it, or they wished to show its similarities, which they found strange too. Later there came those to whom Australia was home, who tried to express it in the best way they could, using methods they had studied abroad or learned from others who had been abroad. Lastly there has arisen a new kind of painting often owing little to anything obviously Australian, permeated by ideas that have been spread around the world by modern techniques of communication yet moulded by minds formed in an Australian background.

To complicate the whole scene two general trends run side by side through all other classifications. One of these consciously seeks to unite art with Australiana: it looks longingly to the past, to the pioneer and his gumtree and to subjects that pertain to the colonial days or to such present-day phenomena as can be isolated as peculiarly Australian. The other looks out to the world of which Australia is only a part, and tries to unite with an international art, or more specifically, with European or American art.

The earliest artists, usually loosely classified under the heading 'Colonial' include surveyors and explorers (Cook himself was no mean picture-maker), convicts — especially those transported for forgery which is, of course, an artistic pursuit — and those settlers who came with backgrounds that inclined them to paint, either as amateurs or, more rarely, as professionals. The bulk of their work was landscape, for the exciting thing about the new land was its difference from the homeland and this could best be conveyed graphically. Portraits were few, being outside the scope of surveyors, and still lifes of this period are rare.

Naturally the artists followed the style that was fashionable in their mother-country when they left her, and this was Romanticism. It sought to follow Nature, and though at first sight this appears the same as Realism, there were several important differences. 'Nature' here is spelled with a capital N. It is not just the nature of botany and zoology but Nature personified — a grand all-pervading force, indifferent to man but with a life of its own. In Australia it has sometimes been thought of as the 'Spirit of the Bush' — especially in the nineteenth century. It was proper to express this by exaggerating such things as the height of hills and trees, the rugged character of the country, and the drama of contrasts.

Romanticism also postulated the artist as somehow superior to ordinary mortals, more gifted and closer to genius. While there are few examples of this in colonial painting, the tendency to use watercolour and etching is a product of this belief in so far as an artist would be equally capable in any medium. The sentimentality of nineteenth century art which is repellant to the twentieth century also derives from Romanticism and is, of course, very evident in early Australian painting.

When the population began to rise sharply with the discovery of gold and improvement in trade, an increasing number of young people devoted themselves to art and proposed to live on the proceeds. Art schools of various kinds appeared, teaching well-established methods and, naturally, unsympathetic to such innovation as was appearing abroad. At length, however, rumours of progress and change reached Australia through new arrivals and returning students. Young painters gathered around these informed artists and gradually a new sophistication came about. The principal figure from overseas was Louis Buvelot, a Swiss, who had wandered about the world seeking a better climate for the sake of his health. He profoundly influenced those young Australians who were drawn towards painting, encouraging them to study their subjects through their own vision.

Two of Buvelot's admirers became important in transmitting new ideas and enlarging the horizons of those who had not travelled: Tom Roberts in Melbourne and Julian Ashton in Sydney. Ashton founded the Sydney Art School, an institution in which many influential artists have since been taught; Roberts became the leader and inspiration of a group which established a series of artists' camps around Melbourne where the members worked at weekends or full time, according to their other commitments. The camp at Heidelberg gave a name to a whole movement, now known as the Heidelberg School or as Australian Impressionism.

It was hardly Impressionism as invented in France, though several technical innovations were common to each: one was the rapid sketch-like character of the works—for each purported to show an instant of time—another was the emphasis placed on capturing the first impression of the subject; it was painted 'on the spot', so there could be no working-over or underpainting in the studio (though sacrifices of principle had to be made when the canvas was large).

But the features which lifted the Heidelberg School above mere painting were not technical. A conviction that a new art was emerging raised the participants to great heights of emotional excitement. Their landscapes glow with the vision of a wonderful world exalted beyond any plebeian account of the ground and growth that lay before them.

Frederick McCubbin, Arthur Streeton and Charles Conder, besides Roberts himself, were the principal figures of the movement. Their first exhibition consisted for the most part of works painted, through the artist's poverty, on cigar-box lids which, since they measured only nine inches by five inches, caused the show to be known as the '9 × 5' exhibition.

Although the new form of painting attracted much attention, few of its proponents were able to make a living from their art; one by one they left Australia, some to study and seek an audience abroad, some never to return. The earlier excitement slowly died, and with its departure painting settled down to a worthy competence only occasionally enlivened by sparks of originality.

For a while, in the twenties, Max Meldrum provided a sensation by preaching through his art school a gospel of strict tonal painting. His theories were in strong conflict with those of the Heidelberg School and between them these two outlooks provided much of the basis of Australian Art before reports of European post-impressionism began to permeate art schools in the thirties.

By then a few artists had already made tentative experiments in this manner, mostly based on reproductions and books from abroad. In Melbourne a school was founded by George Bell and Arnold Shore to teach the post-impressionist philosophy and methods and the movement gave birth to a group which eventually became the Contemporary Art Society. In Sydney similar developments were associated with Julian Ashton's school and encouraged by such older artists as Roy de Maistre and Roland Wakelin.

At first there was great opposition to these revolutionary methods, seen as a threat by those adherents of older traditions. But the social disruption caused by World War Two helped to develop a greater tolerance and from 1945 onwards a new generation began to advance very different ideas of art, the more readily acceptable since the whole social structure of Australia was changing also.

Sidney Nolan, Arthur Boyd, Leonard French and many others began their careers at this time. Exposed to a flood of prints from overseas, to loan exhibitions freely circulating between the world's principal galleries, and with foreign travel more readily available, the provincial attitude which had acted as a spur to some and a brake to many earlier painters was no longer tenable.

The result is that today the proliferation of movements abroad is mirrored in Australia. 'Local content' is minimized, and with so great a variety of acceptable directions to follow, the young painter tends to change his style frequently. Some of the older painters provide works which can be classified under existing headings but most have followed lines of their own which make nonsense of the labels of the past. We have abstraction, both espressionist and hard-edge; we have Dada and surrealism; we have pop art and op art; in short we live in a rapidly changing, even vacillating, world. The conditions that made for a national or a regional art have gone, and it is unlikely that 'Australian Art' will be an acceptable term in another hundred years.

W. J. Splatt

The measurements of the paintings reproduced in this book are given in centimetres and have been adjusted to the nearest half-centimetre. The titles of paintings follow the form currently used by the owner galleries. Details of the ownership and whereabouts of individual works are included in the caption details.

Colour plates

Short titles only are given here: full caption details accompany the plates. An index to artists will be found at the back of the book.

Conrad Martens 1801–1878

View of Sydney Cove and Fort Macquarie (1837)

Martens was one of Australia's first professional painters and his favourite subject was Sydney Harbour. Indeed the greater part of his time in Australia was spent near its shores. He painted it from every angle: in soft colours, with blue waters and rosy foregrounds, at peace beneath a cloudy sky. The accepted conventions of the Picturesque are always present, helped by Martens' exaggeration of those aspects of the scene that lend themselves to romantic interpretation. Thus, in *View of Sydney Cove and Fort Macquarie* the hills are higher, the sea more blue, the 'noble savages' dramatically silhouetted in the foreground, while a co-operative architect has built Fort Macquarie in the likeness of a crenellated castle. Yet steamships are mixed with the windjammers, for progress has its romantic implications too.

Martens was born in 1801 in London where his father, a German merchant, was at one time Austrian Consul. There was a strong artistic heritage in his father's family and from an early age Conrad and his two brothers, John William and Henry, showed considerable talent. Conrad in particular was skilled in topographical work and studied landscape drawing and watercolour painting with A. V. Copley Fielding.

In 1832 he sailed from England in the *Hyacinth* bound for India via South America. On arrival at Montevideo, however, he met the master of the survey ship *Beagle* which carried Charles Darwin and his party, and as a result joined the ship as a topographical artist.

Martens remained on the *Beagle* for two years while a survey of the South American coast was made; when the work was complete he left the ship at Valparaiso and travelled on to Australia via Tahiti and New Zealand. By the time he arrived in 1835, at the age of thirty-four, he was an artist of considerable ability, and not long after he settled in Sydney he opened a studio.

Plate 1 *View of Sydney Cove and Fort Macquarie* (1837)
Watercolour 31·5 × 47·5
Newcastle City Art Gallery. Gift of Dr Roland Pope 1945

Conrad Martens 1801–1878
Elizabeth Bay and Elizabeth Bay House (1838)

Martens was heir to the English tradition of watercolour painting, and he was at his best in that medium. Romanticism was at its height when Martens arrived in Australia and all his works could be said to belong to this category. However, two years working with Charles Darwin aboard the *Beagle* had taught him to record with exactitude, and while his Australian scenes have romantic overtones, the elements are correctly drawn—though perhaps exaggerated in the interests of the picturesque and the market. So in *Elizabeth Bay* the tree on the left is fantastic in size, the light is directed as though by a spotlight, and the colour adds drama to the view of a great country house on Sydney Harbour over a century ago.

Within a year of his arrival in Sydney Martens had received commissions from several influential patrons, including members of the Macarthur family, and the Surveyor-General Sir Thomas Mitchell. He produced harbour views, inland and mountain scenes, and views of town and country houses. In 1837 he was married to Jane Brackenbury Carter and four years later they built a house at St Leonards on the north shore of the harbour.

Though Martens was a leader of public taste in New South Wales, and created a tradition which other artists were to adopt, his own fortunes were dependent on the slender fortunes of the colony; outside the restricted circle of his faithful patrons he received little support or encouragement.

To supplement his modest income Martens also produced several sets of lithographed views of Sydney and its surrounds—among the most notable being *Sketches of Sydney* (1850–51)—taught watercolour painting, repaired and restored paintings and gave occasional assistance to the architect Edmund Blacket.

Martens never became a wealthy man by following his vocation although, in 1863, he was appointed assistant Parliamentary librarian, a sinecure post which brought him a small but certain income and allowed him time to paint and make sketching tours. He held this position until his death in August, 1878 at the age of seventy-seven.

Represented New South Wales, Victorian, South Australian and Queensland State galleries; Bendigo, Newcastle and Launceston galleries; Dixson gallery and Mitchell Library, Sydney; National Library, Canberra.

Plate 2 *Elizabeth Bay and Elizabeth Bay House* (1838)
Watercolour 44 × 63
Art Gallery of New South Wales

S. T. Gill 1818–1880
Sturt's Overland Expedition leaving Adelaide, 10th August, 1844 (undated c. 1844)

The lively, often humorous sketches of S. T. Gill have made him one of the most popular of Australian 'colonial' artists.

The son of a Baptist minister, Gill was born in Somerset, England, in 1818. His first education was at the Naval and Military Academy in Plymouth where his father was headmaster. Later he attended Dr Seabrook's Academy, also in Plymouth, and went to London to train in draughtsmanship and painting.

When his family migrated to South Australia in 1839, Gill, then twenty-one, was already equipped as an artist, and soon began producing 'views and likenesses'. A great part of his work was the production of records of places and events, usually in line and wash. These were often reproduced as engravings and sent back 'home' by the settlers in the colony. The event here recorded is the departure of Sturt's overland expedition which set out in 1844 to search for the 'Great Inland Sea'. Note the upturned boat on the bullock wagon on the extreme right. We can assume that this is a most accurate record, enlivened by touches of caricature in the spectators. It is this accuracy combined with lively incident which makes Gill at once so valued and so loved.

While *Sturt's Overland Expedition* is one of Gill's finest works, he is best-known for sketches he made on the Victorian goldfields. During the 1850s and 1860s several volumes of these sketches were published in Melbourne; among the most notable, *Victoria Illustrated* (1857), *Victorian Gold Diggings and Diggers as They are* (1852–68) and the *Australian Sketchbook* (1865).

Gill's scenes of ordinary life were the foreruners of much of the work produced by such painters as Tom Roberts, Frederick McCubbin and, much later, Russell Drysdale. Indeed, the art historian Bernard Smith has described Gill as 'the most Australian of all artists'.

In Gill's own lifetime, however, he went comparatively unnoticed. Towards the end of his life he drank to excess and sank into poverty and despair. On 27 October, 1880 he collapsed and died on the steps of the Melbourne Post Office and was buried a pauper.

Represented New South Wales, Victorian, Western Australian and (especially) South Australian State galleries; Bendigo and Ballarat galleries; Dixson gallery, Sydney; State Library, Melbourne.

Plate 3 *Sturt's Overland Expedition leaving Adelaide, 10th August, 1844* (undated *c.* 1844)
Watercolour 41 × 73
The Art Gallery of South Australia

J. Skinner Prout 1806–1876
The Tank Stream (undated c. 1840s)

John Skinner Prout, born in England in 1806 and largely self-taught, worked in watercolours to produce picturesque interpretations of scenes in colonial Australia. In England, he had published a series of drawings but, finding difficulty in supporting his wife and large family, migrated to Sydney in 1840.

Here Prout actively promoted watercolour painting while making a living in various ways: he painted scenery at the Olympic Theatre, lectured on art at the Mechanics' Institute and continued to paint and sketch. Between 1842 and 1844 he published *Sydney Illustrated*, a four-part series of drawings with descriptive letterpress. Later Prout moved to Hobart where he helped organize Tasmania's first art exhibition, held in the chambers of the Legislative Council in 1845. A year earlier he had published *Tasmania Illustrated,* a set of local 'scenes'. He also established a successful school of art and gave lectures which encouraged local interest in painting. From Hobart, Prout journeyed to Port Phillip and Norfolk Island, and in 1847 published *Views of Melbourne and Geelong*.

On his return to England in 1848 he continued to give lectures, and put on exhibition a series of views of convict and emigrant life in the Australian colonies. Two further books, *An Illustrated Handbook of the Voyage to Australia* (1852), and *A Magical Trip to the Gold Regions* (1853) followed. The success of these books enabled him to stage further exhibitions and he was later made a member of the New Water Colour Society. He remained active in the art world until his death in 1876.

The Tank Stream was a little rivulet (long since vanished) that supplied the first settlers on Sydney Cove with water, and Prout chose it to provide one of his typically picturesque views of the colony. It is freer and fresher than paintings he made before he left England. The scenic effect is more important than recorded fact, and the location might easily be Italy, the arches in the background the ruins of a Roman aqueduct. Neither the light nor the vegetation are typically Australian (though the pines may be from Norfolk Island) while the technique is that developed in England by the famous band of watercolour painters which included his uncle, Samuel Prout.

Represented New South Wales and Tasmanian State galleries; Mitchell Library and Dixson gallery, Sydney; National Library, Canberra.

Plate 4 *The Tank Stream* (undated *c*. 1840s)
Watercolour 14×19
Art Gallery of New South Wales

W. B. Gould 1801–1853

Flowers and fruit (1849)

Many of the early paintings of Australia were the work of convict artists—notably Joseph Lycett, John Eyre, Thomas Watling and Thomas Wainewright. One of their number was William Gould, Tasmania's first resident artist, who arrived in Hobart Town in December, 1827 to serve a seven-year sentence for having 'by force of arms stolen one coat'.

Gould was said to have been a porcelain painter at the Spode Factory, but on arrival he was put to work at a brick-field and his artistic background did not come to the notice of officialdom until he forged a bank-note. As a result, in June 1829, he was sentenced to three years at Macquarie Harbour. On the journey there, however, the brig *Cyprus*, carrying Gould and other convicts, was seized by mutineers at Recherche Bay. Gould was among a group which travelled overland to seek help and consequently the severity of his sentence was reduced and he was assigned instead to the Colonial Surgeon, Dr Scott, for whom he painted botanical specimens.

Despite his relative good fortune, Gould committed further offences and was again sent to Macquarie Harbour where he sketched the island's fauna.

In 1835 Gould was given his freedom and for a time worked for the coach-builder Henry Palmer in Launceston before returning to Hobart where he later married. During the next decade he painted many still life studies including fish, flowers and game, but drunkenness, poverty and continual misdemeanours made his life wretched and contributed to his death on 11 December, 1853.

Still life compositions of flowers and fruit have been popular since their introduction by the Dutch in the seventeenth century. An artist such as Gould with, as far as we know, no formal training as a painter but with a background in the Staffordshire potteries, would have had little difficulty in reproducing these subjects, which were common as decorations on various wares by Spode. This accounts for the emphasis on decoration and the absence of real coherence between each object. As might be expected from his background, the artist has a primitive touch; this shows clearly in his portraits, some of which may be seen in Tasmanian galleries.

Represented New South Wales, Victorian and Tasmanian State galleries; Queen Victoria Museum, Hobart; Launceston gallery; Entally National House, Tasmania.

Plate 5 *Flowers and fruit* (1849)
Oil on canvas 66 × 77
Art Gallery of New South Wales. Purchased 1956

John Glover 1767–1849

Patterdale Farm (undated c. 1840s)

The first professional artist of note to settle in Australia was a Leicestershire farmer's son, John Glover. As a child, Glover loved to draw the birds he saw in the fields. At the age of twenty he was appointed writing master at the Free School in Appleby and after studying in London under Will Payne, set up as a drawing master in 1794. His work was subsequently exhibited at the Royal Academy and the British Institution and he was a founder and President of the Old Water Colour Society.

Glover was strongly influenced by the work of the French painter Claude Lorraine, and indeed it is said that he wished to become known as the 'English Claude'. His work became fashionable and brought high prices; in 1820 a permanent exhibition of his work was opened at a gallery he had established in Old Bond Street and his success continued.

He was sixty-three, much-travelled and a comparatively wealthy man, when he decided to migrate to Australia. Perhaps a desire to return to the soil and a wish to help his three sons already in Hobart prompted him to take his family to Tasmania where, soon after his arrival in 1831, he acquired land on the banks of the River Nile, at Ben Lomond. He called his property 'Patterdale' in memory of a favourite locality on Lake Ullswater, Cumberland.

In his last years Glover became absorbed in literature—mainly religious works—though a further collection of his paintings was exhibited in Launceston in 1847. He died at the age of eighty-two.

Glover's work is a curious but delightful amalgam of the skills and knowledge he brought with him from England, and the naive interest and excitement occasioned by the appearance of his new country. Here, in the rolling hills of northern Tasmania, Glover and his sons established 'Patterdale', and he seemingly never tired of recording it and its surroundings.

In this painting Glover remembered Claude as he framed the picture with great trees right and left, threw a shadow from one across the foreground, and flooded the landscape with the golden light of a late afternoon in summer. But here are not the ruins of a past civilization—the subject favoured by Claude—but a new farm in a new world.

Represented Victorian, Tasmanian and South Australian State galleries; Launceston and Ballarat galleries.

Plate 6 *Patterdale Farm* (undated *c*. 1840s)
Oil on canvas 77 × 114·5
Reproduced by courtesy of the owners, Mesdames J. W. Butler and L. Nye

Nicholas Chevalier 1828–1902
Self portrait (1857)

One of the most accomplished men of the arts to visit Australia in the middle of the nineteenth century was the Swiss, Nicholas Chevalier. Born in St Petersburg, where his father was overseer on the estate of a Russian Prince, he was to become poet, musician, composer and linguist.

In this country, however, he is best-known as an artist. As a youth he studied painting for six years under J. S. Guignard in Lausanne and later architecture in Munich, before moving to London in 1851 (he was then twenty-three). It is said that a visit to the Great Exhibition of 1851 inspired him to take up water-colour painting; certainly during his time in London he built up a modest reputation as a watercolourist and lithographer, and in 1852 two of his paintings were exhibited at the Royal Academy. About this time, he also designed a fountain for Osborne House and the setting for the Koh-i-noor diamond in the British crown. Later he went to Rome and continued his studies until it became necessary for him to visit Australia to attend to some investments his father had made.

On arrival in Melbourne in February 1855 he joined his brother Louis on the Victorian goldfields. He had planned to stay only briefly; instead he married Caroline Wilke in 1855 and accepted a job as an illustrator on the Melbourne *Punch*. Chevalier's cartoons for *Punch* were well-received, as was his work in the *Illustrated Australian News*. He devoted much of his time to lithography and introduced the process of chromo-lithography to Australia.

Two years after his arrival in Melbourne, Chevalier painted this self portrait; he was then twenty-nine years old. He reveals his abilities clearly: this is no untrained, inexperienced colonial work. The dramatically-lit face merges with the surrounding gloom in a thoroughly Baroque manner. Rembrandt is immediately suggested as a major influence. The artist appears as sensitive and imaginative, and his social popularity is readily understood. At the same time the acceptance of conventional values and attitudes, also to be seen in *The Buffalo Ranges* (Plate 10) is apparent here. Chevalier was competent, but he was no innovator.

Plate 7 *Self portrait* (1857)
Oil on board 35 × 25·5
Art Gallery of New South Wales. Bequest of Mrs Nicholas Chevalier 1919

William Strutt 1825–1915

Gold Diggers receiving a letter from home (undated c. 1860)

Strutt was among the countless Englishmen caught by the lure of gold. He arrived in Melbourne in 1850 and not long afterwards was one of the first to join the Ballarat gold rush. Although he made a number of drawings of the diggers and diggings, he apparently had little success as a prospector and before long he resumed his original profession of artist.

Strutt was born at Teignmouth, Devon, in 1825, the son of Will Thomas Strutt, a painter of miniatures, and grandson of Joseph Strutt, artist and engraver and author of *Sports and Pastimes of the People of England*. His own training, however, took place in Paris at the École des Beaux Arts under Drolling, Ingres, Delaroche and Vernet. While in Paris he illustrated several books, among them *Sacred and Legendary Art* by 'Mrs Jameson', but eyestrain caused him to abandon this work and he decided to travel to Australia. Here, his health improved and he began to work as a lithographer.

Strutt spent twelve years in Australia, a stay interrupted only by a short trip to New Zealand in 1856, and was one of the first painters to produce 'national subjects' on a large scale. He made portraits of well-known local identities including John Pascoe Fawkner, the co-founder of Melbourne, and produced several canvases depicting aspects of the Burke and Wills expedition.

Here, more than in most paintings, we see Australia through alien eyes. Strutt, an Englishman with extensive training in Paris, paints like any European brought up in the neo-classical tradition. As Roberts did fifty years later, he sought to record history, painting those events that were all around him: *Gold Diggers receiving a letter from home* would have been a common sight.

While there is no positive identification of Strutt as the painter of this picture it appears practically certain that he was. The precise drawing, the flawless foreshortening of the hand and arm and the few but telling accessories (note the photograph among the bundle of letters on the keg) suggest that the painter might have been, as Strutt himself claimed, a pupil of Ingres–one of the world's greatest draughtsmen and in his turn the pupil of David, the great French painter of 'History Pictures', whose compositions are faintly shadowed by *Gold Diggers*.

Represented New South Wales, South Australian and Tasmanian State galleries; Ballarat gallery; Mitchell Library, Sydney; National Library, Canberra; State Library and Parliamentary Library, Melbourne.

Plate 8 *Gold Diggers receiving a letter from home* (undated *c.* 1860)
Oil on canvas 91·5×72·5
Art Gallery of New South Wales

Eugène von Guérard 1811–1901
A view of the Snowy Bluff on the Wonnangatta River (1864)

After twenty years of travel and study in Europe, von Guérard brought to Australia the academic approach to landscape and a passionate desire to record each leaf and rock. His ideal was a truthful account of what lay before his eye, but his eye had formed habits in Europe and the colours of his trees were those of European trees: to him the mountains of Gippsland resembled the Alps. No man can escape from his times, and von Guérard's search for truth, like that of so many others, now appears as the transcription of the Old World over a diagram of the New. Yet this was not apparent to the public of the time, for they, too, still saw through European eyes.

Johann Eugen von Guerard was born in 1811 and spent his early years in Vienna where his father was court painter to Francis I of Austria. Shortly before the boy turned fifteen, however, father and son left Vienna and travelled in Europe, eventually settling in Naples, where the elder later died in a cholera epidemic.

In the early 1850s he joined the members of a French prospecting company and migrated to Australia where he compiled a valuable pictorial record of the Victorian diggings.

From the mid-1850s until 1870 von Guérard travelled for as much as two or three months a year, sketching, exploring and mountain climbing. In 1870 he was appointed the first master of painting at the National Gallery of Victoria, but the degree to which he inspired his students seems slight. He resigned his post and returned to England in 1881.

Represented New South Wales, Victorian and South Australian State galleries; Ballarat and Geelong galleries; Mitchell Library, Sydney; State Library, Melbourne; National Collection, Canberra.

Plate 9 *A view of the Snowy Bluff on the Wonnangatta River* (1864)
Oil on canvas 95 × 152·5
National Gallery of Victoria. Purchased 1965

24

Nicholas Chevalier 1828–1902
The Buffalo Ranges, Victoria (1864)

Like von Guérard, Chevalier brought to Australia his 'European vision'; applied to an Australian subject it won him instant success. *The Buffalo Ranges* took a prize of £200 and was the first Australian work bought for the new National Gallery of Victoria. Its local subject matter made a refreshing contrast to other works exhibited in the gallery. Not only did it show a real landscape, but the foreground contained settlers with a bullock team, a bark cottage, a rustic bridge, a waterwheel of indeterminate function and a possible mine shaft. The local content more than offset the Swiss character of the snow-capped mountains and the curious levels of the streams. It is a dark, drab landscape contrasting strongly with the visions of later artists, but it suited the taste of the period.

Chevalier had turned to oil painting in 1856 but despite the acclaim given to *The Buffalo Ranges*, his work in this medium was not generally successful. In 1867 Chevalier went to New Zealand where he made many of his best-known paintings, some of which he exhibited in Melbourne and Paris. On his return to Melbourne in 1868 his work came to the attention of the visiting Duke of Edinburgh, who invited the artist to join him on HMS *Galatea* on a voyage to Tasmania. The Duke found Chevalier's company so agreeable that he later invited him to remain on board and travel to England with him. On the voyage Chevalier executed 120 watercolours. These were presented to Queen Victoria who, in turn, commissioned several works from the artist, including a depiction of the marriage of the Duke at St Petersburg in 1874. As a result of his regal patronage Chevalier found plenty of work and in 1882 became London adviser to the Art Gallery of New South Wales.

In the latter years of his life, however, Chevalier did little painting. From about 1885 he found it necessary to spend the winters in Spain for the sake of his health. In London he composed music and poetry and maintained a wide circle of friends until his death in 1902.

Represented New South Wales, Victorian, South Australian and Queensland State galleries; Ballarat gallery.

Plate 10 *The Buffalo Ranges, Victoria* (1864)
Oil on canvas 132 × 183
National Gallery of Victoria. Purchased 1864

Louis Buvelot 1814–1888
The Yarra Valley, Melbourne (1866)

The work of Louis Buvelot is seen by many critics as a major influence in the development of what has been called the 'Australian School' of painting. He has been variously described as the 'first important artist to arrive in Australia' and 'the grandfather of Australian landscape painting'. Frederick McCubbin said of him: 'There was no one before him to point out the way. He possessed ... the genius to catch and understand the salient living features of the country'.

Yet Buvelot was over fifty when he arrived in Australia. Born in Switzerland in 1814, he had studied there under Arlaud and Wolmer and in Paris under Flers. In 1834 he went to Brazil; first to Bahia, where he worked on his uncle's plantation, painting in his spare time, and then to Rio de Janeiro where he ran a photography studio. Some of his paintings were shown at exhibitions organized by the Academy of Fine Arts and his work came to the attention of Dom Pedro II, who encouraged the artist and gave him the use of a studio at his palace.

While in Rio Buvelot collaborated with Auguste Moreau to produce three sets of lithographed views which were published in 1843 and 1844. His own work earned him considerable recognition and he was honored for his contribution to the arts.

In 1852 Buvelot returned to Switzerland in search of a more suitable climate. He tried to establish himself as a portrait painter but had little success, and during the next few years he moved around frequently; to Calcutta, back to Switzerland, to the East Indies and India. Finally, in 1864, he sailed for Australia. *The Yarra Valley* was painted two years after his arrival and caused considerable interest when exhibited.

The quiet domestic character of Buvelot's landscapes is very evident in this charming view of cattle grazing on the fringe of the growing city, whose presence in the distance emphasises the rural setting. To us today it is like Claude in reverse: instead of a countryside with nostalgic ruins of a past civilization we are presented with a nostalgic countryside and the seeds of a future devastation, for a busy freeway now covers the scene.

In many ways we see again a touch of Europe, but by Buvelot's arrival the landscape around Melbourne *had* been given a touch of Europe. English-style houses clustered together near green fields in which English cattle grazed. The gum trees are the only certain clues to the country of origin.

Plate 11 *The Yarra Valley, Melbourne* (1866)
Oil on canvas 57 × 71
National Gallery of Victoria. Felton Bequest 1934

Louis Buvelot 1814–1888

The survey paddock (1871)

Buvelot brought with him to Australia thirty years' experience in painting and this shows clearly in his work. Moreover, his introduction of the *plein-air* techniques favoured by the Barbizon school in Europe (much of the preliminary work for his paintings was done outdoors) caused him to have a far-reaching influence on the leading students of his day—Roberts, Streeton, McCubbin—who were to become the leaders of a new movement in Australian painting.

His work was 'discovered' in Melbourne by the influential *Argus* critic, James Smith, who compared it with that of Millet and Corot and by 1869 Buvelot was able to devote his full time to painting. In that year *Summer evening near Templestowe* and *Winter morning near Heidelberg* were purchased by the National Gallery of Victoria and before long Buvelot found himself hailed as 'the premier painter of the colony'. A contemporary critic wrote that '. . . what Corot is to France, M. Buvelot is to Australia'.

During the 1870s Buvelot was active in the Victorian Academy of Arts and formed a close friendship with his neighbour Julian Ashton who was to become the leading teacher of his day. Buvelot himself taught for a time, but by 1884 was forced to give up painting when his eyesight began to fail and his hands were crippled. He died on 30 May, 1888 and was buried in Kew cemetery where a memorial was erected by public subscription.

Unlike his predecessors Buvelot did not seek out the odd and exotic in the Australian landscape. No doubt because of his age he did not often work very far from Melbourne; he chose country that was already settled, and this gives a domesticity to many of his pictures. So while the ghosts of a European vision can be found in his work, there is also a very real vision of Australia.

The survey paddock is primarly the picture of a tree; a magnificent gum painted by a man who has seen an oak. Nevertheless it is a gum and the landscape is that around Melbourne. Although only a small piece of the world is included in the composition we are induced to regard it as part of all space by cunning Baroque devices: the light that pours over the landscape from the right, and the little extensions into remote distance of the views on each side of the tree.

Represented New South Wales, Victorian, South Australian, Queensland and Western Australian State galleries; Bendigo, Geelong and Newcastle galleries.

Plate 12 *The survey paddock* (1871)
Oil on canvas 25·5 × 35·5.
National Gallery of Victoria. Presented by John H. Connell 1914

W. C. Piguenit 1836–1914
Mount Olympus, Lake St Clair, Tasmania (1875)

Although Piguenit's work has a European flavour, he was, in fact, the first Australian-born professional landscape painter of standing.

Piguenit was born in Hobart in 1836 to the English descendants of an old Huguenot family. As a child he received some painting lessons from the Scot, Frank Dunnett, and at the age of thirteen he joined the Tasmanian Survey Department as an assistant draughtsman. He spent twenty-three years with the department, painting in his spare time, but it was not until 1872, when he retired from the department, that he was able to paint full-time.

Piguenit had contributed to exhibitions held by the New South Wales Academy of Arts in the early 1870s and held a one-man show at the Academy in 1875. In 1876 he had his first real success with the sale of *Mount Ida with Lake St Clair*. He contributed mountain scenes to the *Picturesque Atlas of Australia* and in 1880 went to New South Wales and joined an artists' camp at Grose Valley in the Blue Mountains. He later settled in Sydney and became a prominent member of the newly-formed Art Society of New South Wales.

In 1898 Piguenit went to England where his work was included in the exhibition of Australian art organized at the Grafton Gallery, London, by Julian Ashton; he also painted in Wales and had his work shown in London and Paris. In 1901 he returned to Sydney (he was awarded the 1901 Wynne Prize for *Thunderstorm on the Darling*) and the following year was commissioned by the trustees of the Art Gallery of New South Wales to paint Mount Kosciusko. He died at Hunters Hill in 1914, and a condition of his will that all his unsold works should be destroyed was observed.

Despite his lack of any substantial formal training, Piguenit's status as a professional painter is considerable, ranking with that of von Guérard and Chevalier. His work is strictly academic, but he manages to obtain atmospheric effects superior to those of many of his contemporaries. While *Mount Olympus* could be European he does get something of its character, and it must be remembered that the Tasmanian landscape is closer to that of Europe than is the landscape of mainland Australia. The mists rising from the lake to partly veil the mountain are particularly well observed.

Represented New South Wales and Tasmanian State galleries; Geelong gallery; Mitchell Library, Sydney.

Plate 13 *Mount Olympus, Lake St Clair, Tasmania* (1875)
Oil on canvas 69 × 107
Art Gallery of New South Wales. Gift of fifty subscribers through New South Wales Academy of Art

Tom Roberts 1856–1931
Bourke Street (Allegro con brio) (1885-86)

Perhaps more than any of his contemporaries, Tom Roberts worked to promote an 'Australian School' of painting. He became one of the great figures of Australian painting at the turn of the century and remains one of the most popular of all Australian artists.

Roberts was born in Dorchester, England in 1856. When his father died, his mother took the family to join her brother in Australia; they arrived in Melbourne in 1869, when Tom was thirteen, and settled in Collingwood, living for several years under difficult circumstances. In 1870 Tom enrolled in the Collingwood School of Design whose teachers included Thomas Clark, who had studied at the Royal Academy, and Louis Buvelot. Here, in 1875, Roberts won the drawing prize and subsequently enrolled in evening classes at the National Gallery of Victoria where he was to make friends with Louis Abrahams and Frederick McCubbin. The Roberts family was in financial difficulties and to assist, Tom worked for a time in his uncle's leather business, then as an assistant to a Collingwood photographer. He later moved to Richard Stewart's photographic studios in Bourke Street, and it was here, in 1876, that he exhibited (and sold) his first work.

Some of Roberts' work was shown at the International Exhibition in Melbourne in 1880 and received favourable mention from the *Argus* critic James Smith. Encouraged by Clark, Roberts decided to study abroad, and with money from the sale of his pictures and the help of Richard Stewart, he sailed for Europe in 1881.

In *Bourke Street* Roberts came close to those street scenes that occupied Monet and Pissarro. From his upstairs studio on a site close to the present Myer Emporium he looked west down Melbourne's busiest street in the middle of a sunny day. Here is Robert's Impressionism at its best. An astonishingly detailed study is made of the life of the times; shoppers and businessmen, hansom cabs and carriages, big shops and a little kiosk, gas lights and telephone poles, parasols and red-coated soldiers. What material for nostalgia has been provided! Each figure is carefully suggested (in 1890 Roberts added three figures to the left foreground of the painting) but nowhere is detail provided to the detriment of the whole. Having determined the size of his picture, Roberts has exactly calculated the means suitable to the total effect, and kept himself to those means. But the first impression, of a sunny, busy town in a happier age remains the triumph of the painter. (He first titled the work *Allegro con brio*.)

Plate 14 *Bourke Street* (*Allegro con brio*) (1885–86)
Oil on canvas 51 × 76·5
National Library of Australia

34

Tom Roberts 1856–1931

Coming South (1886)

When Roberts returned to Australia in 1885 he made the voyage on the *Lusitania*, sharing a cabin with *Bulletin* editor J. F. Archibald. As was to become his method in many later 'history' pictures, he made numerous studies on the voyage, and in the following year completed this small picture of the *Lusitania* which he called *Coming South*. It is a typical subject picture of its time, with one difference. Ingenuously arranged about the mechanical axis of the ship a variety of passengers await arrival in what is for some a strange land, others their own country. There is nervous anticipation or repressed delight for the spectator to seek out; there is variety of character and grouping; all the stock-in-trade of the academic subject picture.

There is also light. This is no worn depiction of a tired theme; the whole scene is illuminated by a consciousness of light streaming from above, soft outdoor light, the light that was to make a new landscape possible in Australian painting.

For four years Roberts studied at Royal Academy schools and earned modest sums by selling drawings to illustrated magazines, particularly the *Graphic*. During this time he also made a walking tour through France and Spain where he met and talked with some notable painters.

Roberts returned to Australia with new ideas. At first he worked a few days a week for Richard Stewart, his old employer, and found some work as an illustrator. In his paintings, however, he sought to apply to the Australian bush the new approaches to rendering light and colour learned abroad, and a year after his return he and Louis Abrahams pitched a tent at Houston's Farm near the rural settlement of Box Hill, nine miles from Melbourne.

Other artists joined the Box Hill camp and in 1886 the group rented a cottage at Mentone on Port Phillip Bay. It was at this beach resort that Roberts came upon Arthur Streeton at work on a canvas and asked him to join their group.

During this time Roberts was active in art circles and was largely responsible for the formation, in 1886, of the Australian Artists' Association, a group which broke away from the Victorian Academy as a result of a split between professional and amateur painters. (It was also largely through Roberts' efforts that the two societies united again in 1888 to form the still existing Victorian Artists' Society).

Most of his time, however, was spent at his studio in Bourke Street where he was endeavouring to establish himself as a portrait painter.

Plate 15 *Coming South* (1886)
Oil on canvas 64 × 50·5
National Gallery of Victoria. Gift of Colonel Aubrey H. L. Gibson, 1967, in memory of John and Anne Gibson, settlers, 1887

Frederick McCubbin 1855–1917

The lost child (1886)

More than any painter before him, McCubbin understood the Australian bush. The sober colours, so foreign to the European eye; the ordered chaos of the undergrowth; the stillness suggestive of indifference or even, as here, of hostility to the newcomer—McCubbin expressed these in the technique of the 'Australian Impressionists'. In the popular taste of his time he made each picture tell a story: here the distressed child points up the mood of the landscape and the human spectator must take her side, bush-lover though he may be. There is nothing objective in this version of Impressionism: the mood of the scene is the subject, and all else is directed towards its expression.

Frederick McCubbin belonged to the minority of 'Heidelberg School' painters who were born in Australia. The son of a West Melbourne baker, he left school when he was fourteen to work in a solicitor's office, though he managed to attend on one day a week at the Artisan's School of Design in Collingwood. A year later, in 1870, he enrolled for evening drawing classes at the National Gallery school.

The bakery business provided a precarious living for the family and McCubbin was periodically recalled to help out, but his father, realizing his son's talents, apprenticed him to a coach-maker where he painted decorations and crests. Later he was able to take day classes under Eugene von Guerard at the gallery. In 1876 his father died and the business again claimed McCubbin's time but within a year he had met Tom Roberts and re-enrolled at the gallery school.

In 1880 George Folingsby succeeded von Guerard at the National Gallery, bringing innovations which greatly inspired his students, particularly McCubbin. Folingsby encouraged exhibitions of his students' work and at the first of these McCubbin won first prize of £30.

In addition to studying and helping at the bakery, McCubbin, in the company of other artists, painted in the bushland at weekends.

Following Roberts' return from England in 1885 the two linked with Louis Abrahams to establish the artists' camp at Box Hill. McCubbin had a special fondness for the bushland in this area and many of his best-known works, including, probably, *The lost child,* were painted here.

Plate 16 *The lost child* (1886)
Oil on canvas 114·5×72·5
National Gallery of Victoria. Felton Bequest 1940

Tom Roberts 1856–1931

Evening, when the quiet East flushes faintly at the Sun's last look (undated c. 1887)

In 1887 Roberts travelled to Sydney, probably on business for the *Picturesque Atlas*, to which he contributed illustrations. He painted with the group led by Julian Ashton and met the young artist Charles Conder,

Two years later Roberts and the Box Hill group shifted headquarters to 'Eaglemont', an old house overlooking the Yarra River at Heidelberg.

Many of the works produced at 'Eaglemont' formed the basis for the famous '9 × 5' exhibition which, largely through Roberts' efforts, was held in Melbourne in August, 1889. The exhibition was held at Buxton's Gallery in Swanston Street and took its name from the fact that all the works had been painted on small panels of wood nine inches by five inches which were normally used for the lids of cigar boxes.

The exhibition catalogue stated in an 'Address to the Public': 'An effect is only momentary, so an impressionist tries to find his place. Two half hours are never alike, and he who tries to paint a sunset on two successive evenings, must be more or less painting from memory.'

Evening, though painted two years earlier, could almost be a larger edition of a '9 × 5' painting. It has the same forthright character in the execution, and the same peace. The landscape itself, with its ochre hills and olive green trees, is typical of the areas once haunted by the Australian Impressionists. There is, too, the same pleasure in light, but here the light is extremely subtle: the long title describes it perfectly. The little farm houses nestling into the hills without benefit of power lines and the unpolluted landscape evoke in us a nostalgia undreamed of by Roberts.

Plate 17 *Evening, when the quiet East flushes faintly at the Sun's last look* (undated *c.* 1887)
Oil on canvas 50·8 × 76
National Gallery of Victoria. W. H. Short Bequest 1944

David Davies 1862–1939
Golden Summer (1888)

'Eaglemont', the old house which became for a time the 'home' of the Heidelberg School, had a commanding view of the valley of the Yarra. The property had originally been owned by a member of Parliament who had planned a magnificent mansion. However, in the middle of a beautifully laid-out garden, with rare shrubs, there stood only an eight-roomed weatherboard dwelling. Over the years, the property passed through several hands until, in 1888, it was owned by an estate company of which Charles Davies was secretary. Streeton came upon the house while walking in the area and after enquiries, obtained the use of the property. By that time the house was in ill-repair and the garden overgrown.

Streeton, Conder and Roberts 'camped' in the house; they slept on beds made of sacks tied between saplings and at night had only candles for light. Here, to earn money, the painters took students, mainly young women, who attended at weekends. It was a precarious existence but in later years the artists remembered the time at Eaglemont as their 'golden summer'.

David Davies, the brother of Charles, was one of the group which painted regularly at Eaglemont. He is best-known as the painter of a series of lyrical 'nocturnes' and bush landscapes, many of which were set in and around the Yarra Valley at Heidelberg.

Born in Ballarat in 1862 of Welsh parents, Davies studied art at the Ballarat School of Design under James Oldham before coming to Melbourne where he enrolled at the National Gallery of Victoria's school under George Folingsby. *Golden Summer* was painted when Davies was twenty-six, shortly before he left Australia for Paris to continue his studies.

At first there is nothing to associate *Golden Summer* with the artist who was later to paint *A Summer evening* (Plate 39). The stark glare of the midday sun and the colours faded by heat only gradually show their affinities with the subtleties of dusk. Yet here also the subject is the mood of the scene. It is the stillness, the pause, the tension between dark and dark that Davies has painted. Nothing stirs in the heat, save the bullocky and his team: their movement stands as a measure of the quietness. There is no dust because there is no wind. The bleached colours result from the all-pervading sunlight; where there is no sun the shadows are black.

Plate 18 *Golden Summer* (1888)
Oil on canvas 60·5 × 91·5
National Gallery of Victoria. Felton Bequest 1937

G. B. Nerli 1863–1926
Street scene on a rainy night (undated c. 1888)

The Italian painter Nerli spent only four years in Australia but despite his brief stay his influence on the other young painters of the time was considerable. The son of an Italian nobleman and an English mother, he was born in Sienna in 1863 and studied at the Florence Art School under Antonio Ciseri and Muzzioli.

Nerli was a talented student, and when he came to Melbourne in 1885 he brought with him the techniques of European Impressionism. His work, how-ever, did not attract much attention (though he painted several portraits and exhibited at the Victorian Artists' Society) and the following year he moved to Sydney. Here his work, with its free style and *plein air* approach, caused some controversy. Charles Conder in particular, with whom Nerli painted in Julian Ashton's group, greatly admired Nerli's style, and it has been said that the Italian painter 'prepared Sydney for Impressionism'.

From Australia Nerli went to New Zealand. He was Director of the Dunedin Gallery for three years and taught the talented New Zealand artist Frances Hodgkins. Later he visited Tahiti and during his stay there painted a portrait of Robert Louis Stevenson which the author is said to have 'preferred amongst all those made of him by artists all over the world'.

On his return to Europe Nerli established a considerable reputation as a painter. During the First World War he was attached to the Italian Embassy in charge of prisoner of war operations.

He died at Nervi near Geneva in 1926.

More than any other artist painting in Australia at that time, Nerli was known for his broad effects, and many of his pictures depended on the reflection of lights on wet surfaces. His street scenes, based on the early work of the French Impressionist Claude Monet, were imitated by his new friends, especially Conder and Streeton. Although *Street scene on a rainy night* is small it conveys not only the wetness and the cold but some of the magic of shimmering lights and mysterious darknesses, of unknown figures and strange buildings.

Represented New South Wales, Victorian and Queensland State galleries; New-castle and Ballarat galleries.

Plate 19 *Street scene on a rainy night* (undated *c.* 1888)
Oil on board 31 × 23
National Gallery of Victoria. Purchased 1951

Charles Conder 1868–1909
Departure of the 'Orient'—Circular Quay 1888 (1888)

Charles Conder was among the youngest of the Heidelberg painters, and while many of his early paintings depicted the rural settings so dear to his colleagues Roberts, Streeton and McCubbin, he did not, like them, devote himself to portraying the 'Australian-ness' of the landscape. Instead he felt the call of Europe and European movements in painting, and when he left Australia in 1890 at the age of twenty-two he did not return.

The son of a railway engineer, Conder was born in London in 1868 and was taken to India as a child. When he was five, however, his mother died and his father sent him back to England to be educated. It was his father's plan that Charles become an engineer but Conder was unwilling to take up this career and instead, in 1883, he was sent to work for his uncle William Jacomb Conder, an official in the New South Wales Lands Department.

He remained with the department for three years, spending most of the time outdoors in survey camps where he developed his love of landscape painting. About 1887, however, he left the Lands Department and began an apprenticeship as a lithographic printer with the publishers Gibbs Shallard; subsequently he became an illustrator for their paper, the *Illustrated Sydney News,* and contributed regular drawings for the *News* for about seven months at a salary of £2 a week. At the same time, Conder enrolled as a night student under A. J. Daplyn at the Royal Art Society of New South Wales; he spent his spare time sketching in and around Sydney in company with a group which included the illustrators Mahony, Fullwood and Minns.

Conder's *Departure of the 'Orient'* was painted when the artist was twenty, and was bought not long after its completion by the Art Gallery of New South Wales—a considerable compliment for so young a painter. It is an interesting example of the knowledge Conder had of the French Impressionists, for the subject matter has much in common with Manet's *Folkestone Boat, Boulogne,* and the high view-point invites comparison with the series of boulevards by Monet and Pissarro. In this, as in the rain-drenched quay, the influence of Nerli is apparent.

Apart from the subject matter it is the patterning of *Departure of the 'Orient'* that pleases: the grouping of the tiny, dark figures, of the ships on the harbour, and the zig-zag edge of the quay, all contribute to the feeling of excitement.

Plate 20 *Departure of the 'Orient'—Circular Quay 1888* (1888)
Oil on canvas 45 × 52
Art Gallery of New South Wales

Charles Conder 1868–1909
Springtime, Richmond N.S.W. (1888)

In 1887, at the house of the artist, Madame Constance Roth, Conder met Tom Roberts who was then in Sydney on business for the *Picturesque Atlas of Australia*. Later one evening, in a wine shop in Mosman, Conder and Roberts had a long conversation which fired Conder's interest in the work and theories of the Box Hill group of painters. As a result of the talk Conder came to Melbourne the following year to join Streeton and Roberts. He shared a studio with Roberts for a time and painted with the Melbourne group, probably at the Box Hill camp and certainly at 'Eaglemont'.

Painted at Richmond, New South Wales, a month before Conder moved to Melbourne, this delightful little picture has, nevertheless, all the characteristics of the Heidelberg School, for Conder had already thoroughly absorbed the ideas of Roberts. In fact it is understandable that the painting was known for many years as 'Springtime, Heidelberg'. Neither its colour, which sets the mood, nor its subject—greening fields and blossom trees—are particularly Australian, but, of course, the country had been settled for a hundred years.

The skilfully touched-in undergrowth in the foreground is a favourite device with Conder, setting the rest of the picture in space. It adds to the faintly Japanese atmosphere which occurs in a number of ways in his work. He has an instinct for decoration: consider the placing of the trees and figures and—as can be seen in every picture Conder painted—the subtlety of the colours. But before all this look at the picture for the emotions it conveys. Is it any wonder that, later, back in Europe, Conder was to be homesick for the 'golden' days he had left for ever?

Plate 21 *Springtime, Richmond, N.S.W.* (1888)
Oil on canvas 45×60
National Gallery of Victoria. Felton Bequest 1914

Charles Conder 1868–1909
Feeding the chickens (1888)

In the little world of *Feeding the chickens* colour and texture are everything. It might be by Vuillard in its toy-like qualities. The light is curious, casting strong shadows on the child's face and none on the ground; coming from the right on the chimney and from the left on the empty dray. We are far from Impressionism and nearer to Whistler; perhaps Whistler per Nerli. The pattern is made from many small units beautifully studded around the picture. The subtlety of the colour shows the decorative powers which Conder was to exploit in the painting of fans when he returned to England. If Conder's drawing is sometimes open to criticism this picture supplies superlative evidence of his powers as a painter.

Conder spent two years in Melbourne, during which time he attended the drawing classes conducted by Frederick McCubbin at the National Gallery school. He also moved out of the studio he shared with Roberts and obtained one of his own in Melbourne Chambers where, according to a contemporary account, the walls were hung with muslin drapes and silks and the place scattered with sketches by Phil May, Ashton and Nerli.

In 1889 he exhibited two allegorical works at the Victorian Artists' Society and was one of the main contributors to the '9 × 5' exhibition held that year; he showed forty-six paintings and designed the Art Nouveau cover of the exhibition catalogue.

At Eaglemont, during the summer of 1889, Conder produced some of his best Heidelberg paintings, but by the end of the year he had made up his mind to go to Europe for further study. Apparently acting on the promise that an 'Uncle Henry' had made to support him for two years in Paris, he sailed from Melbourne in the *Austral* in April 1890.

Plate 22 *Feeding the chickens* (1888)
Oil on wood 28·5 × 40·5
The Art Gallery of South Australia

Arthur Streeton 1867–1943
'Still glides the stream and shall forever glide' (1890)

Among the works of Arthur Streeton are some of the most popular and best-known Australian paintings. Perhaps more than any of his contemporaries, Streeton's works are full of the blues and golds which he considered to be the characteristic colours of the Australian landscape and which have since come to be so closely associated with the Heidelberg painters.

Born in 1867 near Geelong, the son of a school teacher, Streeton's formal training began part-time at the National Gallery of Victoria's drawing classes. He was then seventeen and had a job working in an importer's warehouse, though he later became a lithographic apprentice.

At the gallery school Streeton met McCubbin and later, at the bayside resort of Mentone, met Roberts who was painting there with McCubbin. The two invited him to join them at the Box Hill camp, and Streeton spent his weekends painting there until the sale of two of his works encouraged him to leave his job at the printing works and paint full-time. Streeton initiated the Box Hill group's move to Eaglemont and subsequently contributed forty paintings to the '9 × 5' exhibition of 1889.

Still glides the stream, showing the Yarra River at Eaglemont, was exhibited at the Victorian Artists' Society in 1890 and McCubbin took Julian Ashton, who was making a visit from Sydney, to see the show. Ashton, a trustee of the Art Gallery of New South Wales, was impressed by Streeton's work, and as a result the gallery purchased the painting for £70. It was the first Victorian painting bought by the Art Gallery of New South Wales and its sale marked the beginning of Streeton's success.

Painted near the camp at Eaglemont soon after the '9 × 5' exhibition, this picture was at first called *An Australian gloaming* but Streeton later changed the title, taking a line from a poem by Wordsworth. This is Streeton at his very best: painting in an ecstasy of delight at the scene before him.

Dusk was a favourite time for the Heidelberg painters; indeed, all over the world the closing of the Romantic period was marked by references to twilight, dusk, moonlight, or evening: perhaps Streeton's first title would have been more appropriate. The soft light as we look over the quiet valley towards the rising moon is all poetry and magic, yet as in all great works the means are simple.

Plate 23 *'Still glides the stream and shall forever glide'* (1890)
Oil on canvas 82 × 153
Art Gallery of New South Wales. Reproduced by courtesy of Oliver Streeton

Julian Ashton 1851–1942

The prospector (1889)

Julian Ashton was one of the most influential figures in the Australian art world in the late nineteenth and early twentieth centuries.

Born in Surrey in 1851 and forced to work as a civil engineer in his youth to help support his family, he studied for five years at the West London School of Art, made illustrations for London magazines and was one of the first students at the Académie Julian in Paris. In 1878 ill-health forced him to seek a better climate and he accepted a post in Melbourne as an illustrator on David Syme's *Illustrated News*. Ashton, however, found Sydney more to his liking and in 1883 took a three-year appointment on the Sydney-based *Picturesque Atlas*. Here he joined the Art Society of New South Wales (he later became its president) and taught at its school. In 1889 the New South Wales Premier, Henry Parkes, appointed him a trustee of the Art Gallery of New South Wales and in this post Ashton was to do much to promote the cause of Australian painters.

His greatest influence, however, began to be felt from 1892 when he established his own school, at first known as 'Julian Ashton's school', later as the Sydney Art School. At the same time he allied himself with a group led by Tom Roberts which withdrew from the Art Society of New South Wales to form the New South Wales Society of Artists; he became president of this society in 1897.

Ashton organized the first major exhibition in London of the works of Australian painters—held at the Grafton Gallery in 1898—and his own students were to include such well-known Australian painters as George Lambert, J. J. Hilder, Elioth Gruner and, in later years, William Dobell and John Passmore. In 1920 *The Julian Ashton Book* was published as a tribute to his work.

Although not one of them, Ashton was sympathetic to the Australian Impressionists and himself painted in the *plein-air* tradition, claiming to be the first in Australia to do so. However, he moved restlessly between various styles, and *The prospector* owes a great deal to Courbet. Apart from the subject and the light, which has the harshness of the Australian sun, it might have been painted in Europe. Its chief value today is in its record of the period: the equipment and clothing of the prospector, and his setting in a deep fern gully.

Represented New South Wales, Victorian, South Australian, Queensland and Western Australian State galleries; Geelong and Newcastle galleries.

Plate 24 *The prospector* (1889)
Oil on canvas 213 × 117
Art Gallery of New South Wales. Purchased 1889

David Davies 1862–1939
From a distant land (1889)

In 1890 Davies left Australia for Paris to continue his studies. On arrival he enrolled at the Académie Julian (where he was to meet his future wife) and studied under Jean Paul Laurens. Later he travelled to England, painting for a brief time in St Ives, Cornwall, before embarking for Australia with his wife in 1894.

On his return Davies went to live at Templestowe, near Heidelberg, where he renewed contact with the other members of the Eaglemont group. Here, during the next three years, he painted some of his best works— including a series of studies of the moon rising over the Yarra valley.

In *From a distant land* we have the Victorian subject picture at its most typical: yet it is still touched by the magic that was to flower so magnificently after Davies' return from Europe three years later. It is indeed tempting to attribute this excursion into a popular genre to the desire to raise money for his journey abroad.

The technique is purely Gallery Tonalism indoors: lit by a window behind the figure is a room in a slab-built hut, scantily furnished and finished, with a splendid still life reminiscent of early American painters. The still figure reads a letter from Home. The postman has just left; he can still be seen through the door, riding through a landscape that is purely of the Heidelberg School: the contrast between the outside and the inside could hardly be stranger.

Plate 25 *From a distant land* (1889)
Oil on canvas 90 × 115
Art Gallery of New South Wales

Frederick McCubbin 1855–1917

Down on his luck (1889)

In 1886 McCubbin succeeded O. R. Campbell as teacher of drawing at the National Gallery of Victoria, and not long afterwards he was able to sell the family bakery business which had made such demands on his time. Three years later he married Ann Moriarty whom he had met at an artists' picnic at Blackburn (she appears as the model in a number of paintings by Roberts and McCubbin) and the couple settled at the suburb of Auburn, east of Melbourne. In the same year he contributed five paintings to the '9 × 5' exhibition.

McCubbin's work at this period continued his series of bush-life studies, painted in the *plein-air* manner and redolent of nationalistic and often sentimental feelings. Unlike the works of Streeton and Roberts which often emphasised the bright light, rich colour and optimism of a 'new' country, McCubbin's subjects frequently sounded a note of hardship and melancholy.

Down on his luck is a typical McCubbin of that period when landscapes, based on the Heidelberg brand of Impressionism, were peopled by figures illustrating some aspect of rural life in the pioneering days. That the figures were prepared in the studio was at first obvious: in later paintings this disparateness is corrected. Here the model—he was Louis Abrahams, a member of the first artists' camp at Box Hill—was posed out of doors, but in a hard clear light very different to that of the bushland setting. This bush is typical of that around Melbourne, and in fact, except during his one trip abroad, McCubbin never painted very far from Melbourne.

Plate 26 *Down on his luck* (1889)
Oil on canvas 114·5 × 152·5
Western Australian Art Gallery. Purchased 1896

Frederick McCubbin 1855–1917

A bush burial (1890)

Again and again we see in McCubbin the tragical aspect of the bush. As his work develops it becomes evident that the bush itself is his true preoccupation. The figures satisfy the need to produce subject pictures but, painting by painting, the landscape assumes more importance. His figures are posed and still, caught in a static moment, and are given a clarity that makes them things apart from their setting (which owes more to Roberts) while the figures have Academic antecedents. The little family here mourning the loss of a member—so isolated that no one else is there to mourn with them—repeats the theme of the struggle of the pioneer that is peculiarly McCubbin's.

Bush burial was exhibited at the Victorian Artists' Society in 1890 and McCubbin took the visiting Julian Ashton to see the show—an act which resulted in the sale of Streeton's *Still glides the stream* which was included in the same showing.

The work was painted at Blackburn, not far from the original Box Hill Camp, where McCubbin himself was to settle for a time four years later, and the scene was painted from life: McCubbin's wife was posed as the grieving mother, and McCubbin went so far as to dig a grave in the blue-gum bushland to ensure the accuracy of his depiction.

Plate 27 *A bush burial* (1890)
Oil on canvas 119·5 × 221
Geelong Art Gallery

Arthur Streeton 1867–1943
Near Heidelberg (1890)

The sale of *Still glides the stream* to the Art Gallery of New South Wales, coupled perhaps with that gallery's interest in the works of Australian painters, prompted Streeton to move from Melbourne to Sydney in 1890.

Near Heidelberg was one of the last paintings he made at Eaglemont before leaving for Sydney. When he painted this work Streeton was possibly at the peak of his excitement at the revolutionary way of painting that was being created by his Heidelberg colleagues, Roberts, Conder, McCubbin, Davies and others. It is difficult when viewing this work not to share their surging optimism and delight in their discoveries. The realization that it has passed to leave only such pictorial mementos behind complicates the spectator's emotions today. 'The woods of Arcady are dead, and over is their antique joy.'

It was Streeton who first pointed out that Australia was blue and gold, and this painting might have provoked the remark. Its colour is no less remarkable than its freshness and the skilled handling of the paint.

Plate 28 *Near Heidelberg* (1890)
Oil on canvas 52 × 39
National Gallery of Victoria. Reproduced by courtesy of Oliver Streeton
Felton Bequest 1943

Charles Conder 1868–1909
Yarding sheep (1890)

Yarding sheep is pure Impressionism of the Australian variety. Here form and structure are negligible: the subject is the heat, the glaring light, the dust haze and the colour—blue and gold, the colours of Australia according to the Heidelberg School. The vague horizon stresses the limitless space and the subject swims in the dust, creating the mystery which is so important an ingredient of that hostility the pioneers found in the Australian landscape. Like all Conder's paintings this is small, yet it contains the feeling of a continent, and in this it is unique in Conder's output. He had little interest in that Australian awareness so dear to Roberts and his friends and he painted around the cities rather than in the true bush.

On his return to Europe from Australia in 1890, Conder first visited Rome and Florence, painted for a time in England, then enrolled at the Académie Julian in Paris where he was later to become friendly with William Rothenstein and Henri Toulouse-Lautrec.

A man of good looks and an easy natural charm, he slipped into a Bohemian life of excess which, together with the effects of a serious disease—believed to have been syphilis—forced him to take a period of convalescence in Algeria. When his health improved he continued to move in those circles of artistic people in London and Paris which included Aubrey Beardsley and Oscar Wilde.

Conder married in 1901 but the state of his health continued to deteriorate; his nostalgic correspondence with his former Heidelberg colleagues in Australia diminished and he spent several spells in sanatoria until his death, in Windsor in 1909, at the age of forty.

Represented New South Wales, Victorian, South Australian, Queensland and Western Australian State galleries; Bendigo, Newcastle, Ballarat and Geelong galleries.

Plate 29 *Yarding sheep* (1890)
Oil on canvas 36·2 × 56
National Gallery of Victoria. Bequest of Mary Helen Keep 1944

Tom Roberts 1856–1931
Shearing the rams (1890)

During his travels in New South Wales in the late 1880s, Roberts twice (in successive shearing seasons) visited Brocklesby Station, near Corowa, in the Riverina, where he made many sketches of Outback life. He took great pains to accumulate the data necessary for *Shearing the rams*, preparing more than seventy studies of shearers—some of which are excellent portraits—and for a time set up his easel in the shearing shed itself.

His approach to the subject was explained as follows:
'... one of the best words spoken to an artist is "paint what you love, and love what you paint", and on that I have worked, and so it came that being in the bush and feeling the delight and fascination of the great pastoral life and work I have tried to express it ... If I had been a poet ... I should have described the scattered flocks on sunlit plains and gum-covered ranges, the coming of spring, the gradual massing of the sheep towards that one centre, the woolshed ... the shouts of the men, the galloping of horses and the barking of dogs as the thousands are driven, half-seen, through the hot dust to the yards ... but being circumscribed by my art it was only possible ... to give expression to one portion of this ... it seemed that (in the shearing shed) I had the best expression of my subject, a subject noble enough and worthy enough if I could express the meaning and spirit of strong masculine labour ... and the great human interest of the whole scene ... I believe ... that by making art the perfect expression of one time and one place, it becomes art for all times and all places.'

Though *Shearing the rams* was completed in Roberts' studio he was careful to make the effect as spontaneous as possible, a virtue he had learned from Impressionism. While he is not altogether successful in this—the two figures on the left are very self-conscious—the general effect is one of great realism in the tradition of Courbet, whose work Roberts had admired in Paris. Here the light does not play the important role that it does in most of Roberts' paintings, save that deep shadow is used to control the composition, masking the background and therefore emphasising the foreground figures by dramatic contrast.

Roberts completed the work in 1890 and tried, without success, to sell it to the National Gallery of Victoria. Instead it was later bought by the stock and station agents Edward Trenchard & Co. for 350 guineas.

Plate 30 *Shearing the rams* (1890)
Oil on canvas 119 × 180
National Gallery of Victoria. Felton Bequest 1932

Tom Roberts 1856–1931
The breakaway (1891)

At the end of the summer of 1890 the camp at Eaglemont disbanded. Conder prepared to return to Europe and Streeton went to Sydney where he was joined the following year by Roberts. Here the two established another artists' camp —Curlew Camp—in a picturesque spot at Little Sirius Cove, near Mosman, on a branch of Sydney Harbour. The whole country at the time was facing an economic depression and Curlew became a haven for artists and others down on their luck.

Roberts and Streeton were not as badly-off as some. For a time they shared a studio in Sydney but later Roberts set up his own teaching studio in Vickery's Chambers, Pitt Street. In 1892 he exhibited in Sydney for the first time at the Art Society of New South Wales and in the same year a portrait, *Eileen*, was among the first of Roberts' paintings bought by the Art Gallery of New South Wales.

When Roberts painted *The breakaway* the concept of Australia as a country in her own right was growing and national feeling stirred local art circles. Roberts was particularly affected, and he influenced his friends too. He became obsessed with the necessity to capture the spirit of the pioneers, although their day was nearly past, and a number of great 'historical' pictures resulted. *The breakaway* is one of the earliest examples. Drought-crazed sheep are being held at a waterhole lest they drown or be trampled in a stampede. At the moment depicted, despite the efforts of the riders and their dogs, the stampede has started.

Roberts' earlier experiences in painting the landscape under the spell of Impressionism as he understood it had served him well. The heat and dust of the Australian Outback permeates the scene; the excitement of the incident is communicated. It is hard to credit that the picture was assembled from notes and sketches, and that the foreground horseman was posed in the studio astride a vaulting horse.

Plate 31 *The breakaway* (1891)
Oil on canvas 137·5 × 168·
The Art Gallery of South Australia

Arthur Streeton 1867–1943

'Fire's on', Lapstone Tunnel (1891)

After moving to Sydney, Streeton spent some time at Curlew Camp and exhibited some of his paintings of the harbour at the Art Society of New South Wales. None was sold and the influential critic, James Green, went so far as to suggest that the works were 'a kaleidoscopic nightmare', contending that '. . . treatment of this kind has no place in an exhibition of finished works of art'.

At about the same time Streeton also began to travel extensively in New South Wales, one of his favourite regions being the Blue Mountains west of Sydney. He wrote to Roberts before one of his trips: '. . . I intend to go straight inland (away from all polite society) and stay there two or three years and create something entirely new and try and translate some of the great hidden poetry that I know is here but have not seen or felt . . .'

'Fire's on!' is the warning cry of workmen about to blast, and the Lapstone Tunnel is in the Blue Mountains. A tragic incident is recorded: the body of a workman caught by the blast is being carried out of the tunnel's mouth. In a letter to McCubbin, Streeton described the atmosphere:

'. . . the ganger cries "Fire, fire's on!"; all the men drop their tools and scatter and I nimbly skip off my perch and hide behind a big safe rock. A deep hush is everywhere—then "Holy smoke", what a boom of thunder shakes the rock and me. It echoes through the hills and dies away 'mid the crashing of tons of rock, some lumps fly thousands of feet sometimes and fall and fly everywhere among the trees . . . All at work once more—more drills, the rock is a perfect blazing glory of white, orange, cream and blue streaks here and there where the blast has worked its force!'

Streeton has been at pains to stress the heat and dust, the scale of the undertaking—note the figures on the hill above the tunnel—and the vast rocks.

'T'is like painting in the "Burning Firey Furnace" ' he wrote, and he has conveyed the idea admirably.

Plate 32 *'Fire's on', Lapstone Tunnel* (1891)
Oil on canvas 184 × 122·5
Art Gallery of New South Wales. Reproduced by courtesy of Oliver Streeton

Arthur Streeton 1867–1943
The railway station, Redfern (1893)

As Roberts did with *Bourke Street* and Conder with *Departure of the 'Orient'*, so Streeton, in *Redfern station*, came very close to Impressionism as developed in France. The effect of the instant is here, the tiny figures suggested by a few brush strokes, the bright misty light and the reflections on the wet street. Reflections such as these were a preoccupation of Nerli, whom Streeton had recently met and admired. There is a brilliancy of both tone and colour, and the feeling for atmosphere that started at Heidelberg, together with a pattern of little black accents that keeps the eye wandering happily from incident to incident.

Streeton divided his time in Sydney between Curlew Camp and his excursions into the interior. He also returned for a time to Melbourne where he worked in Roberts' studio and offered to show *Golden Summer* to the National Gallery of Victoria. Streeton wanted £100 for the painting but the gallery declined his invitation to view the work. Back in Sydney at Curlew Camp he eked out an existence on something like four shillings a week, painting around the harbour, at the beaches and on Circular Quay, and occasionally in the city. *Redfern station* was exhibited with the Art Society of New South Wales in 1893 but was not acquired by the Art Gallery of New South Wales until 1942.

Plate 33 *The railway station, Redfern* (1893)
Oil on canvas 41 × 61
Art Gallery of New South Wales. Gift of Lady Denison
Reproduced by courtesy of Oliver Streeton

Tom Roberts 1856–1931

The golden fleece: shearing at Newstead (1894)

Four years after painting *Shearing the rams* Roberts painted *The golden fleece*, a very similar picture—as indeed it must be, since the interior of one shearing shed is much like another, and shearers use the same movements and postures wherever they work. It was painted at Duncan Anderson's Newstead Station near Inverell in northern New South Wales, and first exhibited in 1894. The work was originally known as 'Shearing at Newstead' but received its symbolic title within four years, presumably at Roberts' request.

The principal difference between *Shearing the rams* and *The golden fleece* is the light, which at Newstead comes blazing in through open walls, and the absence of obviously posed figures. No longer is detail lost in gloomy corners; everything is explicity stated, down to the button on a pocket and the construction of the shed. To this extent Roberts has moved away from Impressionism, although within a year he was to produce *Bailed up* (Plate 35) in which his Impressionist inclinations have returned, perhaps because of the landscape background.

Plate 34 *The golden fleece: shearing at Newstead* (1894)
Oil on canvas 104 × 158·5
Art Gallery of New South Wales

Tom Roberts 1856–1931

Bailed up (1895-1927)

Bailed up purports to show the holding up of a Cobb & Co. coach between Glen Innes and Inverell. Since Roberts was a child at the time of the hold-up, the painting is an example of that reconstituted history so important to Roberts' ideas of recording the pioneering days.

Great care was taken to get the details of the painting right. The story was provided by a friend, Bob Bates, who had been the coach driver and of whom Roberts painted a splendid portrait. The landscape background was painted from a perch Roberts constructed in the trees on a quiet road, as near as could be ascertained to the spot where the hold-up had taken place; the coach, Bob Bates and other men were painted at Inverell, and the canvas was completed at Newstead using more men and horses.

The painting was first exhibited at the opening exhibition of the Society of Artists in 1895, but evidently it did not satisfy Roberts and it was extensively altered later. In June 1928 he showed it again at the Macquarie Galleries. It is said that a different landscape background was substituted, and a second date added—'27. After the second showing Roberts wrote: 'The show went well— all things done in Tasmania were bought, also a six-footer of a "Sticking Up" begun thirty years ago, and which I put a lot of work on during last summer.'

Even with all this reconstruction and change the picture rings true. It appears a simple statement about a commonplace event in the life of the colony. Hot sun shines down on a dry country, the coach has stopped without undue excitement; but for the drawn guns and a log across the road, a party of friends might be meeting in the bush.

Plate 35 *Bailed up* (1895–1927)
Oil on canvas 134·5 × 183
Art Gallery of New South Wales

Walter Withers 1854–1914
Bright Winter's morning (1894)

Although a latecomer to the Heidelberg group, Walter Withers was destined to do most of his painting in the area where the camp was first established. Unlike his colleagues, however, he devoted himself exclusively to landscapes.

Born in Staffordshire in 1854, Withers had studied at the Royal College of Art in London and was a practising artist when he arrived in Australia in 1882. For a while he lived in the bush, but in 1884 he took a job as a draughtsman with William Inglis & Co. and began attending night classes at the National Gallery of Victoria. Later he joined the Melbourne printers Ferguson & Mitchell. Withers had long concentrated on black and white studies, notably portraits (around 1886 he exhibited a series of drawings with the Victorian Academy of Arts) but he also found time to paint in oils, and was a member of the Bohemian Sketch Club. This group, which included Streeton, Abrahams, Phillips Fox and McCubbin, made weekend walks to such spots as Ivanhoe and Templestowe where they painted from nature.

In 1887 Withers returned to England and married; a short time later he moved to Paris where he met Phillips Fox and Tudor St George Tucker. He spent a year studying at the Académie Julian before returning to Melbourne in 1888 to make illustrations for 'Garryowen's' *Chronicles of Early Melbourne*, published by his old employers Ferguson & Mitchell.

Back in Melbourne Withers was a weekend visitor to the Eaglemont camp, and in 1890 was one of the first artists to live at the nearby 'Charterisville' estate where another painters' retreat had been formed.

Bright Winter's morning is a charming piece of Romanticism with an interesting variation on the Impressionist concern with light. Here we find the sun breaking through morning mist, making the foreground sparkle, while the distant hill is ill-visible and pastel-hued. It could be the outskirts of a hundred country towns: the small cottages with addition after addition behind them still abound all over Australia, the crude bridges are to be found on every back road. Even the child wheeling a cart up the hill may still be seen, though her dress would be different today. There is always a simple, matter-of-fact approach in Withers' painting. He never seeks to dazzle us with his achievements and his art is therefore much more acceptable than that of others who may be better endowed but are at pains to remind us of the fact.

Plate 36 *Bright Winter's morning* (1894)
Oil on canvas 61 × 91
National Gallery of Victoria. Bequest of Mrs Nina Sheppard 1956

Walter Withers 1854–1914

Tranquil Winter (1895)

It was in the country around Heidelberg that Withers painted *Tranquil Winter*. He avoids that preoccupation with the brilliant Australian sunlight that is so much a part of his contemporaries' world. He prefers the softer effects of atmosphere, a preference possibly acquired in England. He was twenty-eight when he returned from his European studies and spent some time tramping through the Australian countryside before be recommenced painting. It is no English landscape that he depicts. The quiet, cool paddocks, the pale sunlight, the farmhouse and outbuildings, the greenish sky—all mirror the south of Australia. It is the unpretentiousness of the scene that is so convincing.

In the latter part of his career, Withers spent a good deal of his time teaching and involving himself in various artistic groups. In 1891 he gave painting lessons from his studio in the old AMP building in Collins Street, Melbourne; two years later he moved to Creswick, near Ballarat, where he painted scenes of the goldmining activity and gave open air classes which were attended by, among others, Norman and Percy Lindsay. He became a foundation member of the Australian Art Association in 1912 and was a trustee of the National Gallery of Victoria from 1912 to 1914.

Withers won the Wynne Prize for landscape painting twice: in 1897 with *The storm* and again in 1900 with *Still Autumn*. He died in 1914 at his home in the bushland at Eltham, near Melbourne.

Represented New South Wales, Victorian, South Australian, Queensland, Western Australian and Tasmanian State galleries; Bendigo, Geelong, Ballarat and Castlemaine galleries; University of Western Australia.

Plate 37 *Tranquil Winter* (1895)
Oil on canvas 75·5 × 122·5
National Gallery of Victoria. Purchased 1895

E. Phillips Fox 1865–1915

The art students (1895)

The work of Phillips Fox reveals, to a much greater degree than that of his contemporaries, the influence of French Impressionism. It was an influence shown not only in his manner of painting but in his choice of subjects, for while Phillips Fox painted the Australian landscape his paintings are more truly characterized by their preoccupation with sunlight and water, beautiful women, flowers and food.

Phillips Fox was born in Fitzroy, Melbourne in 1865, the son of a photographer. He began his art studies under Folingsby at the Melbourne gallery school, where he won the landscape prize, and in 1887 he went to Paris to study for two years. There he studied at the Académie Julian and the École des Beaux Arts and in 1890 exhibited at the Old Salon; one of his teachers in Paris was Gérome, whose dictum '. . . in painting the first thing to look for, is the general impression of colour' had appeared on the catalogue of the Melbourne '9 × 5' exhibition.

In 1891 Phillips Fox returned to Melbourne. He held a successful exhibition in 1892 and together with Tudor St George Tucker established the Melbourne Art School where the Impressionist ideals and *plein-air* approach were taught. The two also conducted a summer school for painters at 'Charterisville', the old mansion not far from the original Heidelberg group's headquarters, which was to become the centre of an artists' colony for five generations of Australian painters.

The art students was first exhibited at the Victorian Art Society in 1895 but Phillips Fox could find no buyer and the work was still unsold at the time of his death twenty years later.

Five students are painting from life in this exquisite picture, and their teacher has painted them; the setting is the school that Fox and Tucker conducted from 1893 to 1902 (depressions tend to spawn art schools).

The work is beautifully arranged, the varied near-verticals rising through the picture to burst into heads, like flowers on their stems, without the slightest suggestion of straining for effect. The complete naturalness is responsible to a great extent for the charm of the scene: it is hard to remember that every line, tone and colour has been selected and arranged by an act of will. The subdued colours are quite realistic: they could be photographic if their harmony was not so perfect. Notice, too, the intent gaze of each girl as she seeks the likeness of the invisible model, and the corresponding marks on the canvas. It is a little piece of life made perfect.

Plate 38 *The art students* (1895)
Oil on canvas 183 × 114·5
Art Gallery of New South Wales

David Davies 1862–1939
A Summer evening (undated c. 1896)

Davies made a considerable contribution to landscape painting with the magical twilight scenes he painted around Templestowe during the sojourn between his first visit to Europe and his eventual permanent residence there. When studying in France in the early 1890s he undoubtedly saw Impressionist paintings, and these have influenced the surface of his paint which in *A Summer evening* lays a carpet of colour over the canvas. The colours are muted, the tone unobtrusive, but the form is unexpectedly solid. His academic training has not been lost, but neither is it allowed to interfere with the mood.

This haunting personification of Nature is the true subject of these paintings by Davies. He is very much of his period, which dreamed of dim landscapes imbued with a Spirit. Here is a great deal more than 'Nature, as she happens to be', or 'Truth to Nature'. For a brief period the artist felt one with the cosmos, and he can transmit his emotion.

In 1897, three years after his return to Victoria, Davies again decided to go to England. Shortly before, he had moved to the Melbourne bayside resort of Cheltenham and produced some fine seascapes, but he had found no real market for his paintings locally. In London Davies' work was included in the 1898 Australian exhibition at the Grafton Gallery and he subsequently went to live in Cornwall where he spent twelve years. He was not to return to Australia. In ill-health and seeking fresh inspiration for his work, he went to France, settling in Dieppe. Periodically his work was shown at the Royal Academy in London, at the New English Art Club and the Paris Salon. In the final years of his life he returned to England where he died in 1939.

Represented New South Wales, Victorian and South Australian State galleries; Ballarat gallery.

Plate 39 *A Summer evening* (undated *c*. 1896)
Oil on canvas 71·1 × 91·2, mounted on hardboard
Art Gallery of New South Wales

George Lambert 1873–1930

A bush idyll (1896)

George Lambert was born in 1873 at St Petersburg where his father, an American, was working as an engineer. Lambert's father died before his son was born and when Lambert was two years old the family went to live in Wurtemberg, Germany, where they stayed for six years before moving to Somerset, England.

In 1887 (when George was fourteen) the Lamberts migrated to Australia. Mrs Lambert's uncle, Robert Firth, worked a station, 'Eurobla' in New South Wales, and here Lambert developed his passion for painting and drawing (especially horses) while employed as a station hand.

At the same time he began to contribute cartoons of bush life and bush characters to the Sydney *Bulletin*. In 1888 he got a job as a grocer's clerk in Sydney and shortly afterwards began taking evening lessons from Julian Ashton to whom he had been introduced by B. E. Minns, a fellow artist on the *Bulletin*. Before long Lambert was able to make a living from his illustrating and about 1896 he became a full-time student at Ashton's school.

In that year *A bush idyll* was shown at the Society of Artists' exhibition and was bought by the Art Gallery of New South Wales. Three years later Lambert's *Across the blacksoil plains* was one of the outstanding works at the Society's exhibition and was sold to the trustees of the gallery for 100 guineas.

Painted when the artist was twenty-four, *A bush idyll* shows Lambert's debt to Julian Ashton, whose most spectacular pupil he was, as well as the influence of those *Bulletin* artists with whom he worked. The curious way in which the background is merely suggested around the edges, while the centre of the picture is very sharp and clear, is an illustrator's technique to be seen in the *Bulletin* of the time. The colour scheme, too, is peculiar, being superimposed on the subject rather than derived from nature. Decoration is always a prominent part of Lambert's pictures.

Plate 40 *A bush idyll* (1896)
Oil on canvas 48×78
Art Gallery of New South Wales

Frederick McCubbin 1855–1917
On the Wallaby Track (1896)

To be 'on the Wallaby Track' means to be tramping from place to place seeking work. Although the studies for this canvas were probably made at Box Hill and Blackburn, the painting was executed at the bayside suburb of Brighton; this, no doubt, explains the coastal tea-tree and the character of the other vegetation. Impressionism of the French variety is clearly evident. In fact, three of the dominant influences on McCubbin meet here: the *plein-air* painting of the Heidelberg School, the urge to celebrate the legend of the pioneering days, and the increasing awareness of Impressionism as developed in France. There is less conflict between the painting of the figures and that of the landscape: McCubbin is finding his true concern, which will be with landscape itself.

At the time he completed *On the Wallaby Track*, McCubbin was living at Brighton where he had moved with his wife a year before. The painting was first exhibited, however, in New South Wales at an exhibition held in 1897 by the New South Wales Society of Artists. The critical reaction to the work was favourable and it was purchased from the exhibition by the Art Gallery of New South Wales. The following year the painting was shown in London at the exhibition of works by Australian artists held in the Grafton Gallery and organized by Julian Ashton.

The McCubbin family moved home frequently, though they never lived very far from Melbourne. In 1900 McCubbin made a visit to Tasmania and on his return settled for a while in the inner suburb of Carlton before moving to Macedon, north-west of Melbourne, where he found the local bushland a new source of inspiration. He was active in the Victorian Artists' Society and in 1902 was again elected president (a position he had held in 1893) for a two-year term.

Plate 41 *On the Wallaby Track* (1896)
Oil on canvas 122 × 223·5
Art Gallery of New South Wales

Arthur Streeton 1867–1943

'The purple noon's transparent might' (1896)

For Streeton, the wide vista of the Australian landscape was to become his personal version of that exaltation of nationhood that had led Roberts and McCubbin to paint the pioneers. Here, on the upper reaches of the Hawkesbury River, New South Wales, he found ideal subjects. The broad, smooth river running gently through fertile plains ringed by blue hills offers an image of Nature at peace. In theory, at least, the pictures of the Heidelberg School were objective: they presented Nature as she was, although an emotional involvement is always evident. In *The purple noon's transparent might* another factor appears— Streeton is consciously playing to an audience. The pure joy of creation is marred by realization of the necessity to earn a living. But this is still a brilliant summing-up of a mood of Nature, and the delight is still present.

To paint *Purple noon,* Streeton climbed a hill which had an expansive view of the valley of the Hawkesbury. Here he built a shelter to protect himself from the sun and erected a large canvas held in place by stakes driven into the ground to form an easel. He painted during the day and returned to his camp at night.

The purple noon's transparent might was shown at Streeton's first one-man exhibition in Melbourne late in 1896. Streeton took his title from a line of Shelley's and wrote at the time that he had worked 'with a kind of artistic intoxication with thoughts of Shelley in my mind'.

The response to the painting was immediate and favourable and it was purchased for £150 by the National Gallery of Victoria. The success of the exhibition prompted Streeton to go to England the following year in search of a wider audience for his work. He met with only a moderate recognition, however, and in 1907, returned to Australia where he held three exhibitions which proved that his popularity in his own country had not waned.

Plate 42 '*The purple noon's transparent might*' (1896)
Oil on canvas 122 × 122
National Gallery of Victoria. Reproduced by courtesy of Oliver Streeton
Purchased 1896

Tom Roberts 1856–1931
Portrait of Florence (1898)

Roberts' portraits, especially those of women, would prove him a painter of the first rank if all his other work had been destroyed. Usually about life size, and usually of the head only, they thoroughly deserve to be described as 'jewels'. The colours are fresh and delightful, even after three-quarters of a century, the personalities live and the arrangement is invariably interesting. In this picture of 'Florence' notice how crisp and direct is the brushwork on the collar and blouse, how subtly the texture varies on the face where greater detail is demanded; how the veil covers the face without obscuring it in any way. And lastly observe how all these parts add up to the splendid portrayal of a real individual.

By the late 1890s Roberts was regarded in many circles as the best portrait painter in Sydney, and during the last years of the century he spent a good deal of his time on portrait work, his subjects including such notables as Sir Henry Parkes, Viscount Hampden and Earl Beauchamp.

In 1900 he was commissioned to paint a huge canvas depicting the opening, by the Duke of Cornwall and York, of the first Commonwealth Parliament, held in the Melbourne Exhibition Buildings in January, 1901. The work incorporated 250 individual portraits and was unfinished when Roberts left for England in 1903 to complete the job at the Imperial Institute. It was subsequently exhibited at the Royal Academy but was not a success and it left Roberts physically and mentally drained.

Roberts remained in London and continued to paint; his work aroused little interest, although after 1910 he occasionally exhibited at the Royal Academy and the Paris Salon. He visited Italy twice and during World War One served with the RAMC at Wandsworth Military Hospital.

After the war he returned to Australia, held successful exhibitions in Melbourne and Sydney, and settled at Kallista in the Dandenong Ranges near Melbourne. Roberts' first wife died in 1928; later he married an old family friend and for a time lived in northern Tasmania where he painted the local landscape. He died at Kallista in 1931 and at his own request was buried in the churchyard at Illawarra near his wife's home at Longford, Tasmania.

Represented New South Wales (31 works), Victorian, South Australian, Queensland, Western Australian and Tasmanian State galleries; Bendigo, Geelong, Ballarat and Castlemaine galleries; National Collection, Canberra.

Plate 43 *Portrait of Florence* (1898)
Oil on canvas 66 × 38
Art Gallery of New South Wales. Florence Turner Blake Bequest Fund

John Longstaff 1862–1941

Gippsland, Sunday night, Feb. 20th, 1898 (1898)

John Longstaff was one of Australia's most fashionable and prolific portrait painters in the early years of the twentieth century, though he never restricted his work to this field. Born in Clunes, Victoria, in 1862, he first studied art at the National Gallery of Victoria's school under George Folingsby. In 1887 his painting *Breaking the news* won him the first travelling scholarship awarded by the gallery and the following year he went to Paris with his wife to further his studies. Here, during a dinner with the expatriate Australian painter John Russell and the French sculptor Auguste Rodin, it was agreed that he should study at Fernand Cormon's school where he was subsequently to meet Toulouse-Lautrec.

Longstaff's wife was unhappy in Paris and after three years returned to Australia. Her husband, however, remained there until 1894 when he went to England; in London he moved in respectable and influential circles, often visiting the home of former *Bulletin* artist Phil May where the other guests included Melba and Tosti. Longstaff gave a few lessons in painting but soon began to receive commissions for portraits. Late in 1894, however, he decided to return to Melbourne.

Gippsland, Sunday night depicts a scene on 20 February, 1898 when disastrous fires swept parts of eastern Victoria. The picture, painted after Longstaff's return from London, is typical of his few subject pictures which treat the Australian scene. He visited the country devastated by the bushfires, working up the big picture from sketches. It has all the drama of the topic, and if it seems a little conventional in its presentation, we must remember that this was long before colour photography and television made us sophisticated and even callous; it stood up well enough in its period. Then, Realism applied to such a theme meant accurate reporting but no unpleasantness. Longstaff's experience of the academic tradition in Paris and London exerted a strong influence on the picture.

Plate 44 *Gippsland, Sunday night, Feb. 20th, 1898* (1898)
Oil on canvas 143·5 × 196
National Gallery of Victoria. Purchased 1898

John Longstaff 1862–1941

Henry Lawson (1900)

Longstaff had returned from London in 1894 to find the country suffering the effects of a depression and he was at first forced to take work designing advertisements. His reputation as a portrait painter, however, was well-known and before long he obtained commissions to paint portraits of a number of leading figures including the Lord Mayor of Melbourne, the Chief Justice of New South Wales and the writer and poet Henry Lawson.

Longstaff could by that time (1900) produce a likeness with great facility and for the next forty years portraits of the great formed a major part of his work. His portrait of Henry Lawson, then aged thirty-three, shows a conventionally posed young man, attractive in appearance, with the eyes of a poet and fine creative hands. Like most portraits of the time the background is dark, but unlike them it carries the subject's name and the date in large Art Nouveau letters.

In 1900 the trustees of the National Gallery of Victoria commissioned Longstaff to make a large historical painting depicting the arrival of the explorers Burke, Wills and King at their camp at Cooper's Creek. The painting was to be made in London under the terms of a grant made by a leading Melbourne surgeon.

After the completion of the work (a huge canvas measuring nine feet by fourteen feet) in 1907, Longstaff remained in London. He became a leading and highly fashionable portrait painter, whose subjects included Queen Alexandra, Edward VII and the Prince and Princess of Wales; he was prominent in society, exhibited at the Royal Academy and for a time was London adviser to the Art Gallery of New South Wales.

In 1911 Longstaff visited Australia briefly to see his parents. He was commissioned as a war artist in France during World War One and at the end of hostilities settled in Melbourne. He was president of the Victorian Artists' Society in 1924–25 and in 1925 won the Archibald Prize—an award he was to gain on four further occasions within a decade. He was appointed a trustee of the National Gallery of Victoria in 1927 and the following year became the first Australian painter to receive a knighthood. He died in 1941.

Represented New South Wales (22 works), Victorian, South Australian, Queensland, Western Australian and Tasmanian State galleries; Bendigo, Geelong, Ballarat and Castlemaine galleries; universities of Melbourne and Sydney; Australian National War Memorial, Canberra; National Collection, Canberra.

Plate 45 *Henry Lawson* (1900)
Oil on canvas 91·5 × 78·5
Art Gallery of New South Wales

HENRY
LAWSON
1900

Hugh Ramsay 1877–1906
Jeanne (1902)

When Hugh Ramsay died at the age of twenty-nine Australia lost one of her most brilliant and promising painters. Like Longstaff he is best known today for his portraits and like Longstaff his work was moulded by his studies in Europe.

Ramsay was born in Glasgow in 1877 and brought to Australia when he was a year old. Educated at Essendon Grammar School, his first studies in painting were begun when he was eighteen, under L. Bernard Hall and Frederick McCubbin at the Melbourne gallery school, where he won the students' prize in 1896, 1898 and 1899. In the latter year he was an unsuccessful applicant for the travelling scholarship (it was won by Max Meldrum) but at the suggestion of Longstaff he went to Paris anyway and enrolled at Colarossi's studios, and later at the Atelier Délécluse, where George Lambert, with whom he had travelled from Australia, was a fellow student.

Ramsay was greatly influenced by Velasquez and in company with Lambert frequently copied the Spanish master's works in the Louvre. His own talent, however, was indisputable; in the 1902 exhibition at the New Salon four of the five works he submitted were accepted—a rare accolade for a young unknown artist.

The same year Ramsay moved to London where his work was exhibited at the British Colonial Exhibition and the Royal Institute Galleries, attracting much critical interest. Already, however, he had contracted the tuberculosis which was to cause his early death, and in need of a restorative climate he returned to Melbourne.

Jeanne was painted in Paris, where Ramsay had been studying. He had particularly admired the works of that master of tonal painting, Velasquez but he was also influenced by Manet and Whistler. In *Jeanne* the tonal method is predominant, though the arrangement of the model owes something to Whistler. The mood is quiet, the pose is expressive of patient watchfulness. This is helped by the arrangement, strictly frontal in a very shallow space, though slightly asymmetrical, with the minimum of accessories: floor, curtain and chair. But few observers will look at the surroundings. What grips the imagination is the character revealed in the face. It is extraordinary that this young man of twenty-five should be able to paint the woman to come in the face of the child. Ramsay is lifted far above his contemporaries by his great gift of sensitivity.

Plate 46 *Jeanne* (1902)
Oil on canvas 129·5 × 89
National Gallery of Victoria. Lent by Mrs J. Wicking

Frederick McCubbin 1855–1917

The pioneer (1904)

This large triptych contains a magnificent landscape, and
is arranged as three episodes in the life of a pioneer. We
see him arriving on his selection with a covered wagon in
the rear and his bride in the foreground meditating on
the strange new life while he prepares the fire. Then the
land is being cleared; a little cottage hints at the begin-
nings of comfort, and his wife has a child in her arms.
These two scenes prepare us for the third, the pioneer at
the grave of his wife: in the distance a city is established.
In this, one of his last big pictures with figures, McCubbin
moves closer still to Impressionism. The landscape, and
even the figures, are now flecked with colour.

The pioneer, painted at Mount Macedon where McCubbin
was living at the time, was exhibited in an unsuccessful
one-man exhibition which McCubbin held at the Athen-
eum Gallery in Melbourne in 1904. The following year
he re-worked the painting, adding the distant view of
Melbourne in the background of the last panel, and
exhibited it at the Victorian Artists' Society.

McCubbin hoped that the painting would be bought
by the National Gallery of Victoria but his negotiations
were difficult and prolonged and it was not until 1906,
following the death of one of the trustees who had
opposed the purchase, that the gallery agreed to buy the
work for 350 guineas.

McCubbin was now able to take advantage of the
long-awaited opportunity to study in Europe. His students
at the gallery school presented him with a purse of
sovereigns, the Victorian Artists' Society gave him a
farewell party, and in 1907 he sailed for London to spend
a year travelling and studying the old masters.

Plate 47 *The pioneer* (1904)
Oil on canvas: tryptich 225 × 86, 225 × 122·5, 225 × 86
National Gallery of Victoria. Felton Bequest 1906

100

Hugh Ramsay 1877–1906
The sisters (1904)

Ramsay returned from London in 1902 and in the four years that remained of his life he is said to have completed about twenty full-length portraits in Melbourne. Among the most successful was his portrait of David Mitchell, father of Dame Nellie Melba, whose own portrait Ramsay had commenced in London but abandoned when ill-health forced him to return to Australia.

Despite his increasing weakness, Ramsay worked with fervour and energy, completing such notable works as *The sisters* and the equestrian portrait *Dr Sutherland* before his death in 1906. In 1918 the Melbourne Fine Art Society held a memorial exhibition of his work.

In *The sisters,* unlike *Jeanne,* the bravura we associate with Sargent is evident—it would even be dominant were it not for the heads. In spite of the great areas of white and near-white that by themselves could almost form an abstract painting, we find our attention held by the two Edwardian ladies. The great personal achievement of Ramsay is again demonstrated. He could look into his sitters and find a personality which he made clear by means far more subtle than superficial resemblance. Even the poses reflect the characters revealed in each face. The arrangement in three-dimensional space is adequate, but not of real interest to the painter. The two-dimensional pattern is of greater importance; the textures are used as means to an end, but the end is always the remarkable insight into the subject.

Represented New South Wales, Victorian, South Australian, Queensland, Western Australian and Tasmanian State galleries; Geelong, Bendigo and Castlemaine galleries.

Plate 48 *The sisters* (1904)
Oil on canvas 125·1 × 144·8
Art Gallery of New South Wales

Hans Heysen 1877–1968
Sunshine and shadow (1904–5)

Indisputably the best-known and most admired painter of the Australian eucalypts, Heysen was the first Australian artist to capture the true beauty and majesty of these native trees.

Although he was born in Germany in 1877, Heysen was brought to Australia when he was only six years old and grew up near Adelaide where his parents had settled. When he left school at the age of fourteen he worked for a time for a hardware dealer at Norwood, and studied at night at James Ashton's Adelaide School of Arts.

Heysen was just twenty when a group of four Adelaide businessmen who recognized his talent sponsored him on a trip to Europe. In 1898 his work was awarded gold and bronze medals by the Royal Drawing Society of London and the following year he began his studies in Paris where he attended the Académie Julian under Jean Paul Laurens and Benjamin Constant, the École des Beaux Arts under Leon Bonnat, and Collarossi's where he took drawing at night. Later he went on to Italy where he spent a year and studied in Florence, then to England and Scotland. He exhibited at the Paris Salon in 1902 and returned to Australia in 1903.

Before clearing, a great part of the continent consisted of endless plains or gentle hills covered by forests of gum trees in every stage of growth and decay, rising from a red and gritty soil through a mat of fallen leaves, bark and grass, interrupted by shallow, dry water-courses. Here the predominant colours are red, brown and yellow, with the cooler colours of the leaves of the blue-gums.

Stark realism is the aim: no concessions are made to any theory of art. The painting is a witness to Heysen's devotion to its subject, and the intensity of his vision transmits to us this same involvement with the gum-covered plains.

Plate 49 *Sunshine and shadow* (1904–5)
Oil on canvas 176·5 × 114·3
National Gallery of Victoria. Reproduced by courtesy of David Heysen

George Lambert 1873–1930

Equestrian group (1905)

In 1900 Lambert won the first travelling scholarship awarded by the New South Wales Society of Artists and set off to study in Paris. On the voyage from Australia Lambert and his wife, the former Amy Beatrice Absell, met and befriended Hugh Ramsay who was to be Lambert's fellow student at Collarossi's school and later at the Atelier Délécluse.

In 1901 Lambert went to London where he exhibited at the Royal Academy, sent work to the New Salon and continued to contribute illustrations to the *Bulletin* in Sydney. In 1907 he was elected an associate of the New Salon.

Towards the end of World War One Lambert was commissioned as a war artist with the Australian Light Horse in Palestine. His drawings, paintings and sculptures were shown at the exhibition of war art at the Grafton Gallery in 1918 and many are now housed in the Australian National War Memorial, Canberra.

Lambert returned to Australia in 1921 to find himself hailed as a 'leader of the art world'. The following year he was made an Associate of the Royal Academy and for almost a decade he was to remain an influential figure in Australian painting and in the artistic life of the country generally. After his death in 1930 the New South Wales Society of Artists organized a fund to purchase many of his works.

Lambert's two sons achieved fame of their own; Maurice as a sculptor and Constant as a composer and writer on music.

Equestrian group was painted in Paris while Lambert was under the influence of the tonal painting of Velasquez. Even the pose of the child (the artist's elder son, Maurice,) is derived from Velasquez. It is typical of Lambert that he makes a grand gesture: he had the more flamboyant of great masters always in mind. Only in his many war paintings was he completely objective, and they are the better for it. Yet *Equestrian group* is one of his best pictures. While there is a bravura about it, this is not so evident as to distract from the other qualities: a sensitivity towards the subject matter and the handling and the novelty of the composition, all beautifully balanced.

Represented New South Wales (46 works), Victorian, South Australian, Queensland, Western Australian and Tasmanian State galleries; Bendigo, Geelong, Newcastle, Ballarat, Mildura and Castlemaine galleries; Mitchell Library, Sydney; Australian National War Memorial (105 works), Canberra; National Collection, Canberra.

Plate 50 *Equestrian group* (1905)
Oil on canvas 127·5 × 101·5
Art Gallery of New South Wales. Gift of the artist

Rupert Bunny 1864–1947

A Summer morning (undated c. 1908)

Bunny was probably the first Australian-born painter to achieve fame outside his own country. Born in St Kilda, Melbourne, the son of a Supreme Court Judge, he studied civil engineering, then architecture, at Melbourne University before abandoning his courses to enrol at the Melbourne National Gallery school; he studied first under Eugène von Guérard, then under George Folingsby.

In 1884 he went to Europe with his father, studying for a time at the preparatory school of the Royal Academy then moving to Paris where he became a pupil of Jean Paul Laurens. In 1888 Bunny's work was exhibited at the Old Salon and in 1890 his paintings began appearing at the New Salon. In that year he became the first Australian artist to gain an honorable mention at the Old Salon exhibition (with his painting *Tritons*). During the next decade Bunny painted works with religious themes and did illustrations for magazines. His paintings, influenced by the Art Nouveau and Pre-Raphaelite movements, gained considerable critical acclaim and in 1900 he was awarded the bronze medal at the Paris Exposition Universelle.

After his marriage in 1902 to Jeanne Morrell, daughter of a French army colonel, he turned increasingly to scenes in which women were the central feature. He held several one-man exhibitions and in 1904 the first of three of his paintings was acquired by the French Government for the Musée du Luxembourg.

Bunny's long residence in Europe, especially France, led him toward ways of painting quite different to those developing in Australia among his contemporaries of the Heidelberg School. His style can only be called eclectic, combining as it does elements of Manet and Monet, Courbet and Whistler, with many links with other painters of the time.

His large pictures are exhibition pieces. He yearned for a commission to paint a mural but none was offered. However, he painted many huge compositions with Biblical or mythological themes in addition to those such as *Summer morning*, which measures seven feet by six.

Bunny excelled in his pictures of women; tender, graceful, sympathetic portrayals of a leisured class: the Arcadian world of the Impressionists rather than the Workers of the Realists. The figures move gracefully across the canvas or relax elegantly in genteel pursuits. In *Summer morning* the dark and light patterning reminds us of Manet, the brushwork of Courbet, and the reflected light on the sleeve of the standing figure hints at Bunny's knowledge of the theories of Monet and the Impressionists.

Plate 51 *A Summer morning* (undated *c*. 1908)
Oil on canvas 223 × 180·5
Art Gallery of New South Wales

Hans Heysen 1877–1968

A lord of the bush (1908)

On his return from his European studies in 1903, Heysen set up a school of drawing and painting in Adelaide, although his income from this source was extremely modest. In 1904 he married Selma Bartels, daughter of the Lord Mayor of Adelaide, and his *The coming home* was bought by the Art Gallery of New South Wales. In the same year he won his first Wynne Prize with *Mystic morn*, which was subsequently bought by the Art Gallery of South Australia.

But it was not until 1908 when he held a successful exhibition in the Guild Hall, Melbourne, that Heysen's financial situation showed signs of improvement. Up till then the return from his painting had been small indeed: on one occasion he had sold fourteen works for a total of fifty shillings. From the sales at the Melbourne exhibition, however, Heysen received £800, and it was with this money that he purchased a 150-acre property at Hahndorf, in the Mount Lofty Ranges near Adelaide. It was to become his permanent home and the setting for some of his best-loved works.

The following year *Summer* won him his second Wynne Prize and for the first time Heysen was able to look forward to a period of financial security.

Heysen is a remarkable example of single-minded devotion to one ideal. Whereas most artists of his period vacillated between Australia and Europe, and between landscapes and subject pictures, Heysen settled in Hahndorf and spent the rest of his long life painting the surrounding landscape. The Adelaide hills produce magnificent gum trees, and Heysen has become famous with the Australian public for his treatment of them. Unfortunately his imitators have built his methods into a formula, and it is not always easy to see his work through unprejudiced eyes. *A lord of the bush* is a portrait of a tree obviously painted by one who loved it. It is one of his earlier works, and in oil—he used both oil and watercolour—and his draughtsmanship was superb.

Plate 52 *A lord of the bush* (1908)
Oil on canvas 134·5 × 104
National Gallery of Victoria. Felton Bequest 1908
Reproduced by courtesy of David Heysen

J. J. Hilder 1881–1916
The crossroads (1910)

Jesse Jewhurst Hilder was born in Toowoomba, Queensland, and educated at Brisbane Grammar School. At sixteen he took a job with the Bank of New South Wales, working at branches in parts of Queensland and New South Wales. From 1904, when he was living in Sydney, he studied at night classes under Julian Ashton, using a pseudonym for fear that his employer would not approve.

He married in 1909, when he was twenty-eight, but he had already contracted tuberculosis and in the same year his poor health forced him to resign from the bank.

Hilder was to spend the rest of his life painting. He was a prolific worker but the comparatively low prices he received for his paintings forced him to live in near-poverty. In 1907 he had sold twenty-seven works at an exhibition held by the New South Wales Society of Artists and the following year sold another fourteen; during the next six years the art dealer Adolf Albers helped him sell more than 270 works. Ironically, the popularity of his paintings increased after his death in 1916 and works which had originally been sold for five guineas were sold again for 350 guineas.

Hilder's mastery of watercolour is remarkable in view of his isolation from other painters in the medium. While many young ladies were producing genteel water-colour pictures of picturesque subjects in the early years of this century, very few artists in Australia made serious contributions to the art, since watercolour was usually considered a poor relation of oil paint. Nevertheless, it had been a significant part of the Romantic movement of the nineteenth century, and Hilder's work must be seen as one of the last manifestations of Romanticism.

His pleasant landscapes just avoid being merely pretty: they always verge on the sentimental, the colour is appealing, the subjects nostalgic. Yet mere prettiness is avoided by a fine sense of colour; the apparent subject is not the real point of the picture, which is an arrangement of forms in space, despite the atmospheric effects of light. And those qualities peculiar to watercolour are wonderfully exploited.

Represented New South Wales, Victorian, South Australian, Queensland, Western Australian and Tasmanian State galleries; Bendigo, Geelong, Newcastle, Ballarat and Castlemaine galleries.

Plate 53 *The crossroads* (1910)
Watercolour 69·8 × 49·5
Art Gallery of New South Wales. Dr George A. Brookes Bequest

J·J·HILDER
1910

E. Phillips Fox 1865–1915
The arbour (undated c. 1911)

During the 1890s Phillips Fox produced a number of landscapes of Heidelberg and Eaglemont though at the time he was best-known as a teacher.

In 1901 he was commissioned by the National Gallery of Victoria under the Gilbee Bequest to paint a large canvas depicting the landing of Captain Cook at Botany Bay, and in accordance with the terms of the bequest went to London the following year to complete the work, for which he received £500.

In London, in 1905, he married the artist Ethel Carrick, a former Slade student, and after travelling through Europe the couple settled in Paris, where, in 1908 Phillips Fox was elected an associate of the New Salon.

The arbour, painted during Phillips Fox's sojourn in France, is a picture that illustrates his debt to the French Impressionists, and especially to Renoir. He displays the same love of dappled sunlight and the glow of light reflected from surrounding objects, and the subject matter could have been assembled from the works of Renoir himself. Like all the Impressionists he draws on a leisured life in which it is always a summer afternoon, gently happy. There is nothing exotic about his work, nor is there anything particularly Australian about it. *The arbour* is a conventional conversation piece: the children pause in their diversions, the ladies serenely look on and a gentleman pours coffee.

The arbour is painted in broad brush-strokes; astonishing when one approaches the canvas: it almost anticipates the poster artists of the twenties. These add to the decorative charm of the whole, for besides its delightful evocation of happiness it is superbly decorative.

Plate 54 *The arbour* (undated *c.* 1911)
Oil on canvas 190 × 230·5
National Gallery of Victoria. Felton Bequest 1916

E. Phillips Fox 1865–1915
The lesson (undated c. 1912)

The lesson was executed three years before the artist's death. A child reads from a book and her mother sits beside her, while the sunny light from the garden filters through voile curtains from the window behind. The colours are pastel; rosy light and grey-green shade; the technique approaches pointillism. There is a charm about every aspect of this painting: the subject, the setting (note the peacock-eyed cover on the couch and the oval-framed portrait on the wall which date the décor); the colour—even the weather.

Phillips Fox was to spend the greater part of his life in France, though he returned to Australia briefly in 1908, and again in 1913 when he carried out a series of commissioned portraits of prominent citizens. Consequently, the greatest proportion of his work shows the French influence, and in fact he was elected a full member of the New Salon in 1910.

Shortly before the outbreak of World War One Fox went to Tahiti, having become deeply interested in the work of Paul Gauguin. When war broke out he returned to Australia, and in Melbourne in 1915 organized an art union to raise money for the purchase of a lorry for the French Red Cross. He had been home only a short time before he died in October 1915.

Represented New South Wales, Victorian, South Australian, Queensland, Western Australian and Tasmanian State galleries; Geelong and Ballarat galleries; National Collection, Canberra.

Plate 55 *The lesson* (undated *c.* 1912)
Oil on canvas 182 × 112
National Gallery of Victoria. Felton Bequest 1925

Max Meldrum 1875–1955
Portrait of the artist's mother (undated c. 1912)

Max Meldrum was born in Edinburgh in 1875 and arrived in Australia when he was fourteen. A few years later he became a pupil at the Melbourne gallery school, studying under L. Bernard Hall and Frederick McCubbin; in 1895 he won the gallery's students' competition and exhibited at the Victorian Artists' society. After transferring to the gallery's painting school he was awarded the travelling scholarship and in 1899 went to Paris where he studied the works of the old masters in the Louvre. By this time, however, he had evolved his own theories about art; an admirer of Velasquez and the Barbizon school, he rejected Impressionism, Cubism and the dominance of colour, in favour of an overwhelming emphasis on tonal values.

After exhibiting with some success in France he returned to Australia and developed an interest in portrait painting. (His work previously had consisted mainly of landscapes.) In 1913 he founded the Meldrum School of Art and two years later published his book, *The Invariable Truths of Depictive Art*.

Meldrum's ideas attracted a band of student followers which included Arnold Shore, Justus Jorgenson and Archibald Colquhoun, though in the mid-twenties he lost some of his following to the teacher George Bell, who denied Meldrum's theories.

Meldrum's *Portrait of the artist's mother* illustrates at one and the same time his theories concerning painting and his ability to transcend them. His belief was that painting consisted of copying the tonal values of the subject, area by area, on to a canvas: when the painted area matched the equivalent area of the subject the picture was finished. A camera could do no less. Yet it was Meldrum's departures from this simple formula that lifted him above his scores of imitators. *Portrait of the artist's mother* is a presentation of those items that matter, with a complete suppression of irrelative detail. The hair and the dress are completely lost in the background: all that remains are the face and a faint suggestion of collar and blouse. Colour is reduced to a beautifully modulated flesh-tint. It is the sympathetic treatment of the beloved features that lifts this painting above the run of Meldrum's work.

Represented New South Wales, Victorian, South Australian, Queensland, Western Australian and Tasmanian State galleries; Newcastle, Ballarat, Castlemaine and Shepparton galleries; National Collection, Canberra.

Plate 56 *Portrait of the artist's mother* (undated *c*. 1912)
Oil on canvas 61 × 49·5
National Gallery of Victoria. Felton Bequest 1913

Frederick McCubbin 1855–1917
Golden sunlight (1914)

In McCubbin's later works, the landscape becomes the subject and figures are subsidiary. He moves, too, much closer to the impressionism of France. The self-consciousness of his early days, the striving for success, has gone, and delightful little landscapes are produced. No longer does he feel the need to celebrate the men of the bush: he is as devoted to Nature as any of the romantics of the nineteenth century, and indeed there is often a little of Turner in his paintings. *Golden sunlight* contains something of the delight that was so important a factor in the Heidelberg paintings. The whole world sparkles: we are back once more in Arcadia, which the Heidelberg painters had left a generation before.

McCubbin was fifty-nine when he painted *Golden sunlight*, and although his work at this time included some of his most delightful paintings, his health was failing. In 1916 Lothian, the publishers, began work on a definitive monograph of the artist's work and McCubbin threw his energies into the project. The critic J. S. MacDonald contributed the foreword to the book, *The Art of Frederick McCubbin*, and the artist compiled his memoirs.

Despite objections from McCubbin's family to his references to his working-class background and the hardships of running the family bakery business, the book was completed shortly before his death at South Yarra in 1917. Afterwards his old colleague Streeton wrote to Tom Roberts: '. . . the dear old prof has painted a fine lot of pictures in Australia, with the real thing in them, and I hope someone may collect and exhibit them all together . . . We shall all miss him very much'.

Represented New South Wales, Victorian, South Australian, Queensland and Western Australian State galleries; Bendigo, Geelong, Ballarat and Castlemaine galleries.

Plate 57 *Golden sunlight* (1914)
Oil on canvas 76 × 115·5
Castlemaine Art Gallery and Historical Museum. Gift of Dame Nellie Melba

Rupert Bunny 1864–1947
The garden bench (undated c. 1915)

Unlike so many artists, Rupert Bunny's work becomes more delicate and sensitive with time. *The garden bench,* much smaller than *A summer morning,* has a freshness not altogether due to its size. Again, pattern has been important to the artist, striped dress contrasting in direction with striped seat; flowered material below, leafy tree above. So naturally are the models posed that we hardly take in the careful placing of the heads, the tensions created by the glance downwards towards the head of the woman sewing and her gaze toward the embroidery. A delicate rhythm of colour combines with the subtle light to place everything firmly in three dimensional space; yet, in accord with the most advanced theories of the time, while space is suggested the canvas nowhere pretends to be anything but flat. And once again we are in that age of eternal springtime and eternal leisure.

In 1911, when he was at the height of his fame, Bunny returned to Australia and held successful exhibitions in Melbourne and Sydney which resulted in the sale of several works to State public galleries.

With his return to France, however, Bunny entered into a less happy period. He became ill and disheartened; the First World War put an end to the era of grace and elegance depicted in so much of his work and, in the post-war years, he turned instead to paintings depicting classical myths and later to landscapes of the south of France.

Bunny had exhibited in Australia on four occasions between 1922 and 1928. In 1932, desperately short of money and worried by the illness of his wife he returned to Australia in the hope of improving his fortunes. In 1933, however, his wife died and he made a final trip to France before settling permanently in the Melbourne suburb of South Yarra where he painted and composed music.

In the early 1940s successful exhibitions at the Macquarie Galleries in Sydney restored his finances, and in 1946 a retrospective exhibition of his works was held at the National Gallery of Victoria—the first loan exhibition of works of a living artist held at the gallery. The exhibition, which included portraits, landscapes, flower pieces and several large decorative compositions, was Bunny's last, and within six months he died.

Represented New South Wales, Victorian, South Australian, Western Australian and Queensland State galleries; Bendigo, Geelong, Newcastle, Ballarat and Castlemaine galleries; University of Western Australia.

Plate 58 *The garden bench* (undated *c.* 1915)
Oil on canvas 72·5 × 60
Art Gallery of New South Wales

Sydney Long 1878–1955
Fantasy (undated c. 1916–17)

The art of Sydney Long is characterized by his love of the decorative and by what has been called his attempt (which in his later years he abandoned) to 'classicize' the Australian landscape.

Born in Goulburn, New South Wales, Long had his first training at the Art Society's school under A. J. Daplyn; later he studied with Julian Ashton and in London. His first major success came at twenty-two when his oil *Tranquil waters* was bought by the Art Gallery of New South Wales.

Long was elected to the first council of the Society of Artists and was its president from 1898 until 1901. In 1907 he joined Julian Ashton as a teacher at the Sydney Art School, remaining at the school until 1911 when he went to England.

In London, where his work was exhibited at the Royal Academy, Long became interested in etching, and was a foundation member and for a time president of the Society of Graphic Arts. On his return to Australia in 1925 he was made president of the Australian Painters-Etchers Society and directed its school for many years. Long won the Wynne Prize twice, in 1938 with *The approaching storm* and in 1940 with *The lake, Narrabeen*. He was a trustee of the Art Gallery of New South Wales from 1933 to 1949 and died in 1955.

No Australian painter accepted Art Nouveau so completely as Sydney Long. Since the renewed interest in that movement many neglected European artists who were influenced by the style have been rediscovered, but few were so wholehearted in its adoption. Art Nouveau was at first applied to furniture and interior decoration, and the primary appeal of Long's pictures is as decorative panels. Quite flat in composition they present their bushland settings as a series of planes, very like conventional stage scenery, together with a strip of figures also forming a plane across the picture. It might be the stage of a theatre—a very shallow stage—that he depicts.

Yet there is something else. He links his ancient subject matter, in which Pan usually presides, to the bush of Australia. This does not take the spectator back to the age of Pan; rather, Pan is brought forward to the present time, and in Long's painting the Australian bush is linked to all the forests of legend.

Represented Victorian, South Australian, Queensland, Western Australian, Tasmanian and (especially) New South Wales State galleries; Bendigo, Newcastle and Ballarat galleries; Mitchell Library, Sydney.

Plate 59 *Fantasy* (undated *c*. 1916–17)
Oil on canvas 127 × 101·5
Art Gallery of New South Wales. Florence Turner Blake Bequest Fund

Penleigh Boyd 1890–1923
Breath of Spring (1919)

Penleigh Boyd was born in England, the son of two well-known artists and a member of one of Australia's most famous artistic families. His father was the New Zealand-born landscape painter Arthur Merric Boyd and his mother, Emma a'Beckett, the granddaughter of the first Chief Justice of Victoria. Both parents had exhibited at the Royal Academy in 1891 during a visit to London.

Penleigh Boyd studied at the National Gallery school under L. Bernard Hall and Frederick McCubbin and painted at the weekends at Warrandyte; he completed his studies in London and was still only twenty-two when, following his parents' footsteps, he exhibited at the Royal Academy.

On his return to Australia in 1913, Boyd won second prize in the Federal Capital Site competition and the following year won the Wynne Prize with *Landscape*. He served with the Mining Corps in the First World War but was gassed and invalided home.

In 1923 Boyd brought to Australia a significant collection of contemporary European painting which included works by Augustus John, Sir William Orpen, Eric Kennington, Gerald Kenny, Algernon Talmage, William Strang and Dame Laura Knight. The exhibition was shown in Sydney and Melbourne, and it was while travelling in connection with the exhibition that Boyd was killed in a motor accident at the age of thirty-three.

The brief career of Penleigh Boyd was devoted to landscape painting, and he had the reputation of being 'the only artist who could paint wattle'. He reveals a remarkable lyrical quality at a time when it was easy to relapse into mannered lifelessness.

Breath of Spring could have been by Whistler, perhaps as a 'Symphony in green and gold', for Penleigh Boyd had the rare ability to make unlikely colours sing, and his sensitivity helped him to escape the banal. He seems to have by-passed the Heidelberg school yet his freshness and the sense of weather and light that permeates his work link him to that 'golden age' of the nineties.

Represented New South Wales, Victorian, South Australian and Queensland State galleries; Bendigo, Mildura and Castlemaine galleries; National Collection, Canberra.

Plate 60 *Breath of Spring* (1919)
Oil on canvas 122 × 153·5
National Gallery of Victoria. Felton Bequest 1919

Elioth Gruner 1882–1939
Spring frost: Emu Plains (1919)

Elioth Gruner has been called 'the last of the Impressionists'. Although he was not a pioneer of technique and, as some critics have put it, 'did well what others had done before him', he was one of the most popular painters of the twenties and thirties.

Born in Gisborne, New Zealand, Gruner was brought to Australia when he was a year old, and was only fourteen when his mother took him to begin evening classes at Julian Ashton's in Sydney. There after a time, his application to his studies earned him the position of Ashton's assistant and the influence of Ashton is evident in Gruner's early work.

His first exhibited work was *Violets*, 'an unassuming flower-piece', which was included in the Spring show of the Society of Artists in 1901. He continued to exhibit with the Society and in 1912 was able to devote his full time to painting. He began making trips to Windsor and Penrith in the Blue Mountains, near Sydney, and the soft light of dawn in the bush landscape became increasingly the central theme of his work. In 1916 he won the Wynne Prize with *Morning light*, the first of a series of paintings which were to make his reputation.

For three years, on and off, he painted in the open from a cottage at Emu Plains, thirty-four miles west of Sydney. *Spring frost* earned him the Wynne Prize in 1919, although shortly after this success he abandoned the 'early light' theme because he felt it had become over-popular.

Spring frost is typical of Gruner's early work. Light was his first preoccupation; especially early morning light, and especially subjects seen against the light. His tonal training contributed to the success of these paintings and so did his technique, which was to cover the canvas evenly with small brush strokes in the manner of Davies, though it lacked the emotional intensity that made a painting by Davies magical. By the time Gruner arrived on the Impressionist scene it was almost over, and he was the last to bring even a minor creative talent to bear on Australian Impressionism.

Plate 61 *Spring frost: Emu Plains* (1919)
Oil on canvas 131 × 178·5
Art Gallery of New South Wales
Gift of F. G. White 1939. Reproduced by courtesy of Perpetual Trustee Co. Ltd

Elioth Gruner 1882–1939
The valley of the Tweed (1921)

In 1921 the trustees of the Art Gallery of New South Wales commissioned Gruner to paint a 'typical Australian landscape'. The result was one of his best-known works, *The valley of the Tweed*; Gruner worked on it for nearly four months and his efforts were rewarded when the painting was awarded the Wynne Prize.

In *The Story of Australian Art*, William Moore described how the artist found his subject:

'. . . Mr Cedric Campbell, of McIntyre Park near Inverell, offered to motor him through the north-eastern corner of New South Wales. They had got near the border of Queensland when the valley of the Tweed spread out before them. On the right was the Border Gate Road, along which the stage coaches once travelled from Sydney to Brisbane. In the distance they could see the township of Murrwillumbah, while away on the right rose Mount Warning, so named by Captain Cook, who described it as "a remarkable sharp-peaked mountain". Here was the subject for what one might term a national landscape, and it was at this spot that the artist camped and painted the well-known picture, "The Valley of the Tweed".'

The valley of the Tweed has all the superficial attributes but none of the fire of Gruner's great Impressionist predecessors. Indeed, when the picture was exhibited in London it drew the criticism of Sir William Orpen; Gruner was wise enough to take heed, and his later works are to a great extent purged of the sweetness that had been replacing genuine feeling for form and surface. It was perhaps his misfortune to work at the end of an era, when others had made the discoveries, and the excitement had gone. However Orpen's words were not wasted: in spite of his resentment Gruner reconsidered his methods, and his later paintings include his best work.

Plate 62 *The valley of the Tweed* (1921)
Oil on canvas 142 × 172·5
Art Gallery of New South Wales. Reproduced by courtesy of Perpetual Trustee Co. Ltd

Norman Lindsay 1879–1969

The merchant of robes (1922)

Norman Lindsay was one of the best-known of all Australian artists, though there is little in his work which is distinctively Australian in character. He was born in 1879 at Creswick, Victoria, into a family which was to be almost wholly preoccupied with the arts: his brothers Lionel, Percy and Daryl all became well known as painters and illustrators, and his sister Ruby worked in black and white.

Lindsay had received some lessons in painting from Walter Withers when the artist visited Creswick, but he had had no real formal training when he went to Melbourne at the age of sixteen to join his elder brother Lionel. Nevertheless, he made a living, and in 1901 got a job as an artist on the *Bulletin* in Sydney.

During the next years Lindsay spent much of his time writing: his most famous children's book, *The Magic Pudding,* appeared in 1918 with illustrations by the author, and he completed the novels *Redheap* and *Saturdee.*

Throughout the 1920s he occupied himself with painting and sculpture. Several of his paintings were included in the 1923 exhibition of Australian art held at Burlington House in London and in 1930 a special edition of the magazine *Art in Australia* was devoted to his work. Lindsay's themes, however, so offended the morals of the time that the magazine was prosecuted for obscenity; the case was dismissed but Lindsay was so disgusted at the commotion he went to America.

On his return he settled at the house at Springwood in the Blue Mountains, west of Sydney, which was to be his home and studio for the rest of his life. He remained a controversial figure almost until his death in 1969 at the age of ninety.

Norman Lindsay's world is very much a dream-world, both exotic and erotic. He has a great deal in common with Watteau. The same misty gardens furnished with the same classical ornaments—urns and balustrades, fountains and the occasional column—are peopled by voluptuous women and leering men, all with maniacal eyes. The compositions are splendidly executed, usually as etchings or watercolours—both fashionable mediums during Lindsay's lifetime. *The merchant of robes* might be from the Arabian Nights. It has little to do with the Australian scene or with the life of the intellect, but it provides an excellent excuse for a demonstration of the artist's highly skilled handling of watercolour.

Represented New South Wales, Victorian, South Australian, Queensland, Western Australian and Tasmanian State galleries; Bendigo, Castlemaine and (especially) Ballarat galleries.

Plate 63 *The merchant of robes* (1922)
Watercolour 44·7 × 41
Art Gallery of New South Wales

Arthur Streeton 1867–1943
The land of the golden fleece (1926)

In 1908 Streeton left Australia for England for the second time; in London he married a Canadian, Nora Clench, and together the couple toured Europe. During World War One he served for a time at the Wandsworth Military Hospital in company with Roberts, and later he was commissioned as a war artist. In 1920 he returned to live in South Yarra near Melbourne.

More exhibitions and more overseas travels followed until, in the late 1920s when Streeton was in his early sixties, he settled permanently in Melbourne. In 1921 he had been made art critic for the Melbourne daily the *Argus* and in 1931 a Streeton retrospective exhibition was held at the Art Gallery of New South Wales. Streeton was knighted for his services to Australian painting in 1937 and retired to his home at Olinda in the Dandenong Ranges, not far from where Roberts had spent his last years. Streeton died in 1943.

Streeton's later years were spent making pictures of the Australian landscape: wide tracks of sunny settled country, here and there a station homestead with cattle or sheep or a windmill tiny in the distance, backed by blue mountains under blue skies with picturesque white clouds. Such a painting is *Land of the golden fleece,* three versions of which exist. It was about the time of this painting that MacNally, the art critic of the *Age,* complained that Streeton's pictures were beginning to show a commercial bias, and indeed, while the concept of *Land of the golden fleece* is grand, and the execution masterly, the old élan is gone.

Represented New South Wales, Victorian, South Australian, Queensland and Western Australian State galleries; Bendigo, Geelong, Newcastle, Ballarat, Mildura, Shepparton and Castlemaine galleries; Australian National War Memorial (56 works), Canberra.

Plate 64 *The land of the golden fleece* (1926)
Oil on canvas 50 × 76·5
National Gallery of Victoria. Reproduced by courtesy of Oliver Streeton
Bequeathed by W. C. Cain 1950

Hans Heysen 1877–1968

Red gums of the far North (1931)

Heysen won the Wynne Prize for landscape nine times;
Red gums of the far North (1931) was his eighth winner.
This truly magnificent watercolour records a quartet of
giant eucalypts growing on the desert fringe. It is impos-
sible to ignore the pathetic fallacy here: these are not
mere trees but the embodiment of such human traits as
nobility and aspiration. They reach out to the blue sky
while grasping the ground firmly, defying the elements
or strange Aboriginal gods. It is the same country that
Drysdale painted later but the approach is entirely
different. Drysdale is concerned with Man helpless in the
face of Nature, Heysen with holding up Nature for
Man's admiration.

Heysen's devotion to the Australian eucalypt never
waned, and he wrote of his favourite subject with something approaching awe:

> 'Its main appeal to me has been its combination of
> mightiness and delicacy—mighty in its strength of
> limb and delicate in the colouring of its covering. Then
> it has its distinctive decorative qualities; in fact, I know
> of no other tree which is more decorative, both as
> regards the flow of its limbs and the patterns the bark
> makes on its main trunk. In all its stages the gum-tree
> is extremely beautiful—first from being a tiny sucker
> with its broad leaves, shooting up like fountains
> answering to the slightest breeze—at middle age it
> becomes more sturdy, more closely knit and bulky,
> yet never losing grace in the movement of its limbs
> and the sweep of its foliage. In its prime it is really a
> magnificent and noble tree . . .'.

Plate 65 *Red gums of the far North* (1931)
Watercolour 48 × 63·5
Art Gallery of New South Wales

136

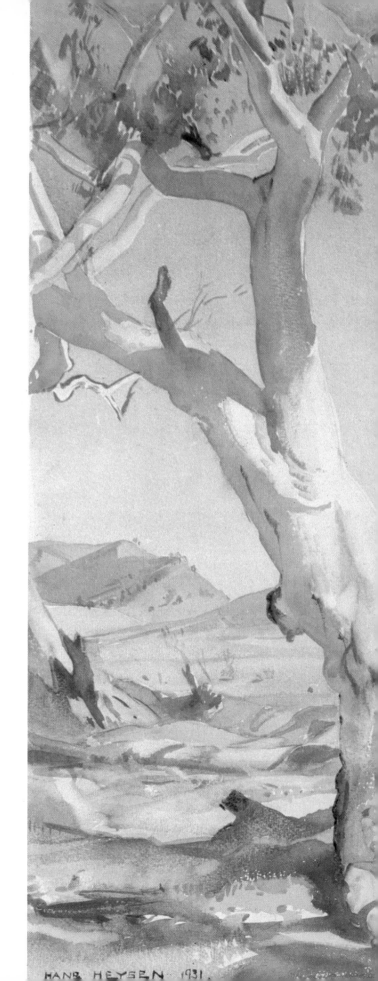

Hans Heysen 1877–1968
The land of the Oratunga (1932)

While so much of Heysen's work is characterised by his homage to the eucalypts of the Adelaide hills, he was also among the first painters to find fascination in the stark forbidding landscape of the interior, in particular, the Flinders Ranges of South Australia.

Heysen's powers were at their height (he was fifty-five) when he painted *The land of the Oratunga* in 1932. Like most of his work it was prepared in the studio from sketches made from nature. It demonstrates his remarkable competency in watercolour which had been a favourite medium since his student days, when the English watercolour school had caught his attention in London. Turner had impressed him most, but De Wint, Cox and Girton had been studied too, and their influence can often be seen in his later work.

There exist a number of versions of this subject in oil as well as in watercolour, besides numerous sketches.

In the year he painted *Land of the Oratunga* Heysen won the last of his nine Wynne Prizes (with *Brachina Gorge*). Eight years later he was appointed to the board of the Art Gallery of South Australia and in 1959 he was knighted for his services to art. He died in 1968 at the age of ninety-one.

Represented New South Wales, Victorian, Queensland, Western Australian, Tasmanian and (especially) South Australian State galleries; Bendigo, Geelong, Newcastle, Ballarat, Mildura and Castlemaine galleries; University of Western Australia.

Plate 66 *The land of the Oratunga* (1932)
Watercolour 48 × 63·5
The Art Gallery of South Australia

138

ANS HEYSEN, 1932.

Noel Counihan b. 1913

At the start of the march (1932–44)

In 1932 there was every inducement for a young man to take a long look at society. What Counihan saw he has never forgotten. His work does not lovingly depict the lyrical bush, the awesome Centre, the golden beaches, nor the affluent nor their properties. He has been close enough to that human misery generated by faults within society itself to be preoccupied with its recording and to take a leading part in protest.

His paintings are Expressionistic, with the short free brush-strokes so revealing of emotion; his colours are dull as befits the subjects, his contrasting tones add drama. *At the start of the march*, begun in 1932 but not completed until 1944, isolates one family in a desolate space edged by a frieze of figures huddled against a wall at the rear, and the assembled marchers on the right. It appears to be a hunger march. The adults are stoic despite their misery, but the child on the left expresses all they do not. Human sympathy for fellow humans is predominant. Counihan's anger is subdued, and far more effective for that.

Social comment has always been an integral part of Counihan's art. His political sensitivity is acute and for many years he made a living from his caricatures and political cartoons. Born in Albert Park, Melbourne in 1913, he was educated at Caulfield Grammar (where he first became interested in art) and sang in the choir at St Paul's Cathedral, Melbourne. After leaving school he got a job as an office boy in a Flinders Lane warehouse and took the evening classes at the Melbourne gallery school. When he was sacked from his job in 1932 (he led a deputation asking for overtime pay) he thought of getting a job as a commercial artist but Victoria was in the grip of the Depression and he could not get work.

Counihan was deeply involved in the political movements of the time, avidly read the works of Marx, Engels, and Lenin, and had brushes with the police as a result of his political activities. For a time he was staff artist on the Melbourne *Guardian* and later worked for the World Trade Union Movement. In the early 1950s he went to Europe and from 1956 to 1960 he studied in Russia; while in Europe his political caricatures appeared in many publications including the London *Daily Mail*. He has exhibited widely in Australia and in London, Copenhagen, Warsaw, Moscow and Leningrad.

Represented New South Wales, Queensland and Western Australian State galleries; Bendigo, Geelong, Newcastle and Ballarat galleries.

Plate 67 *At the start of the march* (1932–44)
Oil on masonite 67 × 59·5
Art Gallery of New South Wales

140

William Dobell 1899–1970
The boy at the basin (1932)

The career of William Dobell—unquestionably the most famous of modern Australian portrait painters—has been marked by both controversy and success. At one time labelled a caricaturist by his critics he went on to win the Archibald Prize three times and to see his paintings sell for record-breaking prices.

Dobell was born in Newcastle, New South Wales, in 1899. As a boy he hoped to become a pianist but by the time he left school painting had become his great interest. For a time he studied drawing at Newcastle Technical College and in 1916 became articled to a local architect, Wallace Porter. At the end of his apprenticeship in 1929 he went to Sydney, worked as an architectural designer, and attended evening classes at Julian Ashton's where the works and teachings of George Lambert were an early influence.

One of Dobell's ambitions in this period was to become a newspaper cartoonist, but Ashton and others dissuaded him and in 1929, after winning the Society of Artists' Travelling Scholarship and several other prizes, he went to London and enrolled at the Slade School of Art to study drawing. In 1930 he won first prize for life painting at the Slade and subsequently went to Holland where he spent three months studying the old masters, particularly Rembrandt, Goya and Daumier.

The boy at the basin is a small picture, painted in London just before Dobell's individuality began to emerge. It is quiet and retiring: nothing is done for effect. Dobell had already begun a study of Rembrandt's works but here we are reminded of other Dutch masters—especially Vermeer with his serene, impersonal vision and his room so beautifully bathed in cool revealing light. Dobell's colours are subdued and delightful, but above all it is his remarkable ability to use paint that makes this work a taste of things to come. Here the texture makes towelling, there it is enamel, now it is wood, now metal, and now flesh, yet it is always paint. The whole is a piece of student work, carefully feeling its way among the possibilities, but what a student! Soon after Dobell painted this canvas his work gained confidence and a more personal style appeared.

The boy at the basin was exhibited at the Royal Academy, London, in 1933 and purchased by the Art Gallery of New South Wales in 1939.

Plate 68 *The boy at the basin* (1932)
Oil on wood panel 40·5 × 33
Art Gallery of New South Wales

William Dobell 1899–1970

The sleeping Greek (1936)

Four years after *The boy at the basin* and while he was still in London, Dobell painted *The sleeping Greek*. Now the texture and the drawing are both freer, the colour less dependent on reality and more evocative.

Dobell now reveals an interest in the people he paints: there is little in *The boy at the basin* to concern us about the model himself, but this 'sleeping Greek' is a particular Greek, a waiter with whom Dobell became acquainted, and who posed for several other pictures. He is peaceful in his sleep despite the artificial light shining strongly on his face. The composition is different in kind. We have not an assemblege of separate objects but one object organized into a painting, the axis tilted not only to indicate sleep but to provide for tensions between contours and an appropriate pattern. The textures provided by the brush-strokes help this pattern but, most important, they reinforce the form while retaining the feel of the material they depict.

Dobell spent ten years in England and Europe, during which he was often forced to take various odd jobs to make a living. In spite of his meagre income, however, he made no attempt to sell his paintings which, by 1936, were to include such now well-known works as *The sleeping Greek, Mrs South Kensington* and *Red lady*. When he returned to Australia in 1938 he brought his paintings with him; they were first shown in Australia at the Society of Artists' annual exhibition in August the following year.

On his return the artist settled in King's Cross. He commenced teaching at East Sydney Technical School in August 1939 and was commissioned to paint a mural for the Australian pavilion at New Zealand's centennial exhibition in Wellington.

Plate 69 *The sleeping Greek* (1936)
Oil on canvas 38 × 33, on masonite
Art Gallery of New South Wales. Gift of the Society of Artists in memory of Sydney Ure Smith 1950

Elioth Gruner 1882–1939
Bellingen pastoral (1937)

In *Bellingen pastoral* we see Gruner at his best. The lessons of the past are learned, and the temptations of the twenties put aside. The countryside is still a little too tidy, the rules have been followed so carefully that they show, but there is a lyricism and a delight in the subject that appeals. We share the peaceful afternoon and the calm routine of pastoral life. It would never do to paint the Australian desert thus, but it suits those parts of the country which, like the English landscape, have been 'patted into shape'. The magic of the Heidelberg painters has gone, but there remains a hint of their dream of 'golden days' which Gruner was just too late to share.

In 1923 the Sydney art journal *Art in Australia* devoted a special issue to Gruner's work and in the same year he went to London to manage an exhibition of Australian paintings (which included eight of his own) at the Royal Academy. When the exhibition closed he travelled in England and Europe, and as a result of his visits to the leading galleries his own style of painting began to change. It has been said that after his return to Australia in 1925, form became more important to him than the effects of atmosphere.

In 1926 Gruner exhibited with the Contemporary Group at the Grosvenor Gallery in company with his colleagues George Lambert, Roland Wakelin and others and two years later his work was shown in an exhibition of contemporary artists of the British Empire at the Imperial Institute in London. Once again he modified his style, returning in some degree to his original preoccupation with the effects of light in the landscape.

Gruner was awarded the Wynne Prize seven times (five times between 1921 and 1939); his work was popular and he was prominent in the Australian Academy of Art and the Society of Artists. He died in 1939.

Represented Victorian, South Australian, Queensland, Western Australian and (especially) New South Wales State galleries; Newcastle, Castlemaine and Geelong galleries; Mitchell Library, Sydney.

Plate 70 *Bellingen pastoral* (1937)
Oil on canvas 62·5 × 75
National Gallery of Victoria. Felton Bequest 1940
Reproduced by courtesy of Perpetual Trustee Co. Ltd

William Frater 1890–1974
The red hat (undated c. 1937)

William Frater was among the first group of Australian painters to come under the influence of the European post-impressionist movement.

Born in Scotland in 1890 he was brought up by an uncle who, when Frater was fifteen, sent him to the Glasgow School of Art. Frater showed an impressive command of technique but after four years he quarrelled with his uncle and set out to follow his younger brother Tom to Australia.

Frater arrived in Melbourne in 1910. Here he met the painter Arnold Shore and worked for a time with a firm which made stained glass windows. In 1911, however, he decided to return to Scotland. After visiting the great galleries in Madrid and Paris he went back to his former school in Glasgow and studied there for a further two years until he resolved to return to Australia.

After being rejected for military service in World War One Frater returned to the stained glass business and was to remain in this craft until World War Two.

At first under Meldrum's influence, Frater later became inspired by reproductions of the European post-impressionists; by the late twenties he had developed his overwhelming admiration of Cezanne. In 1931 he exhibited with Arnold Shore and became a member of the Melbourne Contemporary Group. He visited Central Australia in 1950 and in the same year was elected president of the Victorian Artists' Society. A large retrospective exhibition of his work was held at the National Gallery of Victoria in 1966.

The influence of Cezanne is more apparent in the work of Frater than in that of any other Australian painter. Nonetheless, in all his paintings, there is a strong individuality of a kind that may be thought of as Romanticism. He uses the appropriate modelling through planes of colour but he retains some of the excitement of the subject. His landscapes and portraits give more than a chart of the object before him. In this portrait of his colleague Lina Bryans, herself a painter of considerable talent, space has been flattened to avoid any suggestion of illusionism. The figure however, is stated as a three-dimensional entity; forms make an arrangement in space, and so do the contours. Nothing, however, has been sacrificed to technique or arrangement: it is superb portraiture, conveying not only the appearance but the personality of the model.

Represented New South Wales, Victorian, South Australian, Queensland, Western Australian and Tasmanian State galleries; Bendigo, Geelong and Ballarat galleries.

Plate 71 *The red hat* (undated *c.* 1937)
Oil on canvas 93 × 73
National Gallery of Victoria. Felton Bequest 1943

Russell Drysdale b. 1912

Moody's pub (undated c. 1941)

Russell Drysdale was one of the first painters to discover the Australian 'outback' as a subject; indeed, it has been said that Drysdale's paintings of the desolate fringe of the interior are better known to most Australians than the outback itself.

Drysdale's family had a long association with the land in Australia. Although the artist was born in Sussex, England, in 1912, his father's forebears had been pastoralists in Tasmania, the Riverina and north Queensland since the 1820s, and when Drysdale's family arrived in Australia to settle in 1924 it was accepted that his destiny lay on the land.

After his schooling at Geelong Grammar Drysdale became an overseer on his father's property and it was only by chance that he came to make painting a career. In 1932 he developed a defect in his left eye and was forced to go to Melbourne for treatment. Here he took to sketching to fill in time, and after his work had been shown to Daryl Lindsay and the teacher George Bell their encouragement led him to make a trip to Europe where he subsequently studied both the old masters and the post-impressionists.

On his return to Australia in 1933 Drysdale went back to the land but began sketching in earnest and two years later decided to take up art full-time. He studied under George Bell, and after a second trip to Europe in 1938, worked for a time in a studio Bell loaned him.

Rejected for military service at the outbreak of World War Two, Drysdale took a job managing a country property until, in 1940, he moved to Potts Point, Sydney. Here he began to paint landscapes, taking as his theme the drought-stricken Riverina areas he had seen the year before.

Of all the pictures that Drysdale painted at the beginning of his preoccupation with the outback, *Moody's Pub* is probably the best known. It could be any country town, any country pub. It is hot and dry, the buildings are old and dilapidated, the car has seen better days, and so have the customers.

To this extent the painting is starkly realistic; but more is provided. The elongation of figures, buildings, even the car, produces a tautness that grips the attention in exactly the same way and by using the same methods as did the paintings of Parmigianio three hundred years earlier. To this Drysdale adds heat and desiccation by the use of colour, achieving a total effect that tells the spectator a great deal about life in the outback, and transmitting the emotional impact of a town that endures from day to day, barely hoping for a revival.

Plate 72 *Moody's pub* (undated *c.* 1941)
Oil on wood panel 51 × 61·5
National Gallery of Victoria. Purchased 1942

Roland Wakelin 1887–1971
Richmond landscape, Tasmania (1944)

Roland Wakelin was born in New Zealand in 1887 but in 1912 he settled in Sydney. He studied at the Art Society's classes under Antonio Dattilo Rubbo and in 1917, after several posts as a public servant and ticket-writer, he was employed by the advertising firm owned by Sydney Ure Smith and Harry Julius.

In 1922, when he was forty-five, Wakelin took his family to London where he spent three years working as a commercial artist and studying art in his spare time. On his return to Australia he continued to work in commercial art and paint in his spare time. The critics, however, were largely hostile to his painting, which defied the artistic taste of the times, and it was not until 1935 that he held a really successful exhibition.

Wakelin's careful, intellectual method of composing his pictures owes much to Seurat; his devotion to form, expressed through the modulation of colour, to Cezanne, and although the mood of his painting is very different to that of Van Gogh his colours often reflect the latter's colours. (Wakelin once said: 'Cezanne was the major influence of my life and I once made the mistake of trying to paint as he did.') His work could be summed up as lyrical landscape, bathed in romantic colour and designed in space. His is a gentle decorative art. In *Richmond landscape, Tasmania* the celebrated bridge and the church on the hill have the attraction of ancient monuments, but this is not the point of the picture. It is rather a tribute to the forms of stone, earth, and water, and to sensuous colour.

Represented Victorian, South Australian, Queensland, Western Australian, Tasmanian and (especially) New South Wales State galleries; Bendigo, Newcastle and Castlemaine galleries.

Plate 73 *Richmond landscape, Tasmania* (1944)
Oil on pulpboard 62·8×75
Art Gallery of New South Wales

Albert Namatjira 1902–1959

Glen Helen landscape, (undated)

Albert Namatjira became the first Aboriginal artist to achieve popularity with a wide Australian audience, possibly because his paintings were always executed in the Western manner.

Born into the Arunta tribe at Hermannsburg in the Northern Territory, he worked as a camel-driver, stockman and station hand before turning to the manufacture of carved and painted artifacts. Namatjira was introduced to water-colour paintings in 1934 by the Melbourne artist Rex Battarbee.

On a second visit in 1936 Battarbee took Namatjira with him to Palm Valley and gave him further tuition. As a result, several of Namatjira's works were later shown in Adelaide with an exhibition of Battarbee's paintings; this was followed in 1938 by Namatjira's first one-man exhibition, in Melbourne, at which all forty-one paintings were sold.

European patronage and benevolence, however, proved a mixed blessing for Namatjira. Granted 'Australian citizenship' in 1957, he was subsequently arrested for supplying other Aboriginals (who were not 'citizens') with liquor. Namatjira was sentenced to six months' imprisonment with hard labour. He was released after serving two months of the sentence but died not long after, on the reserve where he had first learned to paint.

It is difficult for the inheritors of Western culture to see Namatjira's landscapes as he himself thought of them. To us both subject and artist are exotic: the country mysterious and hostile to the white man, the Aboriginal artist quite remote from European culture. Yet he is looking at his tribal lands, familiar since birth—looking with the acute vision natural to his race. That he paints the visual equivalent of the actual scene is really the exotic aspect of his work. It would be more natural for him to produce a symbol.

We therefore tend to admire in Namatjira those qualities that he would take for granted, while neglecting those he might hope would be admired. That the colours and forms are strange and romantic, that the atmosphere is so clear as to resemble that of primitive artists: these things are pure accurate reporting. The evidence of great gifts lies in his being able to present these facts in a manner and medium quite foreign to Aboriginal tradition.

Represented South Australian, Queensland, Western Australian and Tasmanian State galleries; Bendigo gallery; University of Western Australia; National Collection, Canberra.

Plate 74 *Glen Helen landscape* (undated)
Watercolour 40·5 × 58·5
Reproduced by courtesy of The Legend Press Pty Ltd, sole publishers of Namatjira's work

Sidney Nolan b. 1917

Death of Constable Scanlon (1945–47)

Although largely a self-taught painter, Sidney Nolan has become one of the very small band of Australian artists to achieve a world-wide reputation. Born in 1917 in Carlton, Melbourne, the son of a tram driver, Nolan had a minimal education and as a young man worked in a variety of unfulfilling jobs. These included making electric signs, designing men's hats and arranging advertising displays.

Although he had begun drawing at the age of six, Nolan's brief training in painting began at Prahran Junior Technical School when he was fourteen and continued when he enrolled at the Melbourne gallery school at the age of nineteen. At neither place, however, did he show any evidence of great talent nor any interest in the kind of artistic training he was receiving.

At twenty-one, Nolan became a foundation member of the Contemporary Art Society. His closest friends were a group of young radical painters and writers who included Albert Tucker, John Perceval, Max Harris, Geoffrey Dutton and John Reed, and in company with the latter three Nolan was later to become a partner in the literary quarterly *Angry Penguins*.

In 1938 he married and decided to spend his full time painting. One of his first major series—a child's dream interpretation of St Kilda and other parts of Melbourne—was completed during the 1940s.

With the outbreak of the Second World War Nolan enlisted in the Army, but was able to continue his painting, and during this time produced a series of 'poetic interpretations' of the Australian bush.

Nolan is above everything else a painter: he thinks in terms of a picture and so deeply feels the implications of his subject that the spectator cannot but be involved too.

His first 'Ned Kelly' series, ignored in Melbourne when first exhibited in 1948, subsequently brought him international fame. Nolan's uncle, Bill Nolan, himself an amateur painter of bush landscapes, had been one of the police troopers who joined the search for the outlaw, and from the time of his boyhood Nolan had a fascination with the story and legends surrounding the Kelly gang. The series patiently deals with the legend episode by episode, but there is nothing patient about the pictures themselves. The Kelly symbol menaces whatever accompanies it; even the landscape backgrounds take the side of the bushranger. In *Death of Constable Scanlon* the trooper falls from his horse like an acrobat, the trees seem to approve, and Kelly stands to one side like a magician whose results are achieved without any apparent effort on his part. This is truly the stuff of legends.

Plate 75 *Death of Constable Scanlon* (1945–47)
Ripolin on hardboard 91·5 × 122
Reproduced by courtesy of the owner, Mrs Sunday Reed

Sali Herman b. 1898

The Law Court (undated c. 1946)

Although he was almost forty before he came to Australia, Sali Herman's understanding of the Australian scene, especially the urban landscape, is remarkable.

Born in Switzerland in 1898, one of a family of eighteen children, he left school when he was fourteen with the idea of becoming a painter. Instead, his parents sent him to a shop to sell gloves—a job which lasted only a few weeks before Herman and his young brother left home and set off for Paris. Here he spent two frugal years working and studying until in 1916 he returned to Zurich; he took further study and exhibited two years later.

Although he was beginning to establish a reputation with his work, Herman abandoned painting when he was twenty-five to become an art dealer. He followed this career for fourteen years until the economic depression in Europe caused him to abandon his business and come to Australia, where his widowed mother had settled some years earlier.

After his arrival in Melbourne in 1937 Herman returned to painting; he studied with George Bell for fourteen months and then moved to Sydney where he managed to sell some of his work. In 1944 he won the Wynne Prize with *McElhone Steps* and during World War Two he served as a war artist in 1945–46. Herman won the Wynne Prize again in 1963 and 1965, and his work was the subject of a monograph by Daniel Thomas in the Australian Art Monographs series published by Georgian House in 1962.

Paintings by Herman hang in Australian legations in the USA and France.

Sali Herman has re-made the old buildings around inner Sydney with his own vision. He sees them through a romantic glow, the 'light that never was', for though some walls are brilliantly lit and others shaded, shadows are rare. The light exists only to create pattern and mood, and the mood is always gay. Yet this is no flat decoration. Herman was a good pupil of George Bell and the pattern of forms is never forgotten, nor is the use of paint to create texture. *The Law Court* has an additional interest, for this is Francis Greenway's building of 1819.

Represented New South Wales, Victorian, Queensland, Western Australian and Tasmanian State galleries; Bendigo, Geelong, Newcastle and Ballarat galleries; Australian National War Memorial, Canberra.

Plate 76 *The Law Court* (undated. *c.* 1946)
Oil on canvas 61 × 81·5
National Gallery of Victoria. Felton Bequest 1946

Russell Drysdale b. 1912
Two children (undated c. 1946)

In the period immediately after his move to Sydney in 1940 Drysdale sold little of his work but by the time the war had ended he had begun to attract attention. His name became familiar to a mass audience for the first time in 1944 when the *Sydney Morning Herald* commissioned him to travel through the west of New South Wales to make line and wash sketches (later published in a series by the newspaper) of the drought conditions. As a result Drysdale's work became increasingly popular and he was an exhibitor at the Macquarie Galleries. Nevertheless, during the late forties he never managed to earn more than about a thousand pounds a year from the sale of his paintings and sketches.

Here, rare among Drysdale's paintings, there is no hint of place. *Two children* is obviously set in the outback, but no distant house, no unpaved street, no stone mountain or waterhole hints at a setting. There is only yellow sand under a dusty sky: the colour suggests aridity but even the light is soft.

The children are monumental, no less figures in a landscape than are works by Henry Moore, and they share his simplicity of form, together with that of Modigliani. This form is suggested by conventional techniques: the teaching of George Bell is still evident.

The children's clear-eyed gaze is watchful but serene, withdrawn and patiently waiting for the artist to finish. But it is the classical serenity of *Two children* that holds the painting in our memory. Drysdale has achieved an image of loneliness that haunts the city dweller.

Plate 77 *Two children* (undated *c.* 1946)
Oil on canvas on composition board 61 × 51
National Gallery of Victoria. Purchased 1946

Russell Drysdale b. 1912
Sofala (1947)

Sofala is a small mining town in New South Wales. Once crowded with life, it died, like so many Australian towns, when the gold ran out, leaving behind monuments to reasonable aspiration. Here are large buildings, empty and stripped or inhabited by those too old to go or content to eke out life on the pension by fossicking in the old workings. Drysdale is on the whole an accurate reporter of the world he watches but there is tension in his burning colour and in his elongated poles and pillars, and the empty windows waiting for someone long dead. No living thing is to be seen, human or animal, not even vegetation. As in so much recent painting Mannerism is come again, and Drysdale has profited from those forms of Surrealism current in the thirties.

In 1947 Drysdale won the Wynne Prize with *Sofala* and three years later held his first one-man show in London. It was a great success and one of his works was bought by the Tate Gallery.

He continued to make journeys into the outback, and following a trip to Cape York in northern Queensland in 1951 he became preoccupied with the situation of the aborigines who were to be the subjects of numerous sketches and paintings during the next decade. In 1958 he joined an old friend, Professor Jock Marshall, on a four-month trip in northern and north-western Australia, and Marshall's subsequent book *Journey Among Men,* containing about fifty of Drysdale's black and white drawings, became one of the most publicised and successful books of its day.

Plate 78 *Sofala* (1947)
Oil on canvas 72 × 93
Art Gallery of New South Wales

Arthur Boyd b. 1920
Irrigation lake, Wimmera (undated c. 1948)

The Wimmera wheat district in the north-west of Victoria is less arid than Central Australia, less lush than Gippsland and the Mornington Peninsula where most of Boyd's earlier landscapes were painted. Vast plains are ringed by low blue hills and crossed by dry creek beds. Here is made obvious the Impressionists' discovery that Australia is gold and blue. It is a habitable landscape: not only crows and cockatoos live here but man and his cattle, with his fences and carts (and his irrigation). Trees, dead and dying, reach to the sky, linking the two vast horizontal planes of earth and heaven, each broken, the one by the curve of the bank and the other by the jagged hills. The landscapes Boyd painted at this period (1945–52) are perhaps his most popular works.

Few Australian artists have achieved such international fame as Arthur Boyd. Together with his contemporary Sidney Nolan, Boyd has been responsible for an unprecedented overseas interest in Australian painting, his exhibitions in London receiving the kind of critical attention which his forerunners of the Heidelberg School so dearly sought and never obtained.

Arthur Merric Bloomfield Boyd was born in Murrumbeena, Melbourne, in 1920. His father was the potter William Merric Boyd and his mother, Doris Gough, was a painter; he was a grandson of the New Zealand landscape painter Arthur Merric Boyd and nephew of the artist Penleigh Boyd.

Appropriately for one born into such a distinguished artistic family, Boyd regularly won the drawing prizes at Murrumbeena State School where he was educated. However, at fourteen he went to work for an uncle in a paint factory, and although he spent several months at night classes at the National Gallery of Victoria's school, he has not had much formal training in painting.

After he had left the gallery school, Boyd went to live with his grandfather on the Mornington Peninsula; he painted here for about two years and when he was nineteen he held his first one-man show of Impressionist landscapes and portraits. In 1941 he joined the Army—serving first as a gunner and later in the Cartography Corps—where he met a fellow artist John Perceval. His contact with Perceval brought him, after the war, to the Contemporary Arts Society whose members included Albert Tucker, Sidney Nolan and John Reed. Partly as a result, Boyd's own style of painting changed, and after the war he produced a series of Expressionist paintings on the theme of war devastation. He married the painter Yvonne Lennie in 1944 and settled with his wife at the Murrumbeena pottery where he worked with Perceval and Peter Herbst.

Plate 79 *Irrigation lake, Wimmera* (undated *c.* 1948)
Resin and Tempera on hardboard 81 × 122
National Gallery of Victoria. Purchased 1950

Sidney Nolan b. 1917

Pretty Polly Mine (1948)

In 1947 Nolan set off to spend a year wandering in northern Queensland and on Fraser Island in the Great Barrier Reef region; during this time he made many paintings of the landscapes and small country towns.

The following year he was married for the second time—to Cynthia Reed, sister of John Reed, his patron and one of his partners in *Angry Penguins*. Soon after, the first series of Kelly paintings, which had been shown in Melbourne without attracting any praise from the critics, were exhibited in Paris; on this occasion, however, they caused considerable interest.

In 1949 Nolan was travelling again, this time in Central Australia—a trip which produced another important series of landscapes.

Nolan's trip through Queensland in 1947 provided two series of paintings, one concerned with the outback, the other with Mrs Fraser, who survived for six months after being wrecked on Fraser Island. The outback pictures are mainly of a building or town, battered by the years and by the weather, curiously evocative in a way different to that of Drysdale. Nolan's surrealism plays some part here: clear and unclear areas are inexplicable save that they strengthen awareness, and some monstrous image floats above—a bird, a photograph, a machine. In *Pretty Polly Mine* it is Polly herself, flying huge over the strange mine machinery which looks rather like a river steam boat stranded in the desert.

Plate 80 *Pretty Polly Mine* (1948)
Synthetic enamel on hardboard 91 × 122
Art Gallery of New South Wales

Sidney Nolan b. 1917
Macdonnell Ranges (1949)

Nolan's Central Australian landscapes are all large—*Macdonnell Ranges* measures three feet by four; all were painted with Ripolin (a synthetic enamel) on Masonite, and nearly all are predominantly red and blue. Light and shade play a limited part—the glare of the tropical sun and the lack of strongly modelled features provide the reason. The world has strong affinities with the Wilderness of the Bible.

In 1951 Nolan visited France, Spain, Portugal and Italy, and after his return was commissioned by the *Courier-Mail*, Brisbane, to make a series of drawings of the drought-stricken areas of northern Queensland. In 1953 he returned to inland Australia with the film director John Heyer before leaving once again for Europe where he spent the next three years.

In 1957 a large retrospective exhibition of Nolan's work was held at the Whitechapel Gallery, London, and by 1960, when his Leda and the Swan series was the highlight of the London art season, leading critics had hailed him as 'one of the outstanding painters of our time'.

Nolan has continued to be an insatiable traveller, visiting South-east Asia, Turkey, India, the United States, Africa, Japan and the Antarctic. These journeys gave rise to further major series including Africa (1963) and the Antarctic. The latter series was exhibited in London in 1965 at the Marlborough Gallery.

In 1974 the artist donated a large collection of his works to the new National Gallery in Canberra.

Represented Victorian, South Australian, Queensland, Western Australian, Tasmanian and (especially) New South Wales State galleries; Ballarat gallery; University of Western Australia.

Plate 81 *Macdonnell Ranges* (1949)
Synthetic enamel on masonite 91·5 × 122
The Art Gallery of South Australia

Lloyd Rees b. 1895
The harbour from McMahon's Point (1950)

Lloyd Rees developed a strongly individual style, starting from a point close to the tradition of the later Streeton. His landscapes are remarkable for a number of characteristics not very evident in the landscape painters around him. He is a superb draughtsman; he has a monumental sense of form—exceptionally so in a landscape painter; he can give drama by the manipulation of tone, without such manipulation ever becoming oppressive; he has a feeling for texture rare in any painter in any period, and more important than all of these, though perhaps because of them, he can show us a piece of the planet Earth as though that is just what it is. He is often classed as a romantic but he is much more than that word conveys.

Lloyd Rees has been drawing and painting for more than seventy years. Born in Brisbane in 1895, the seventh of eight children, he first started to draw when he was six, decorating the lids of his mother's hat boxes. At the Ironside State School near Brisbane he developed his talent for drawing but the chances of him making a living from art seemed so remote that when he left school he went straight to work, first for an insurance office then later for a bank.

At sixteen, however, illness forced him to leave the bank and on his recovery some months later his parents agreed to allow him to enrol in art classes at the Brisbane Technical College. After working for a time at the Government Printing Office, Rees began to receive some commissions and his work came to the notice of the publisher Sydney Ure Smith, who reproduced some of Rees' work in his periodical *Art in Australia*. Subsequently Ure Smith invited Rees to work for the commercial art firm which he ran in Sydney.

Here Rees designed advertisements, and during his spare time began to work in oils. In 1923 he was able to go to Europe for study in Rome and London; after his return in 1924 he married and went to live in a small flat at McMahon's Point overlooking Sydney Harbour. In 1927 he again fell ill and although he returned to commercial art, little of his own painting was seen for seven years. His most recent major exhibition was held in Sydney in 1974, following a trip to Italy and France the year before.

Represented New South Wales, Victorian, South Australian, Western Australian, Tasmanian and (especially) Queensland State galleries; Bendigo, Newcastle, Ballarat and Castlemaine galleries.

Plate 82 *The harbour from McMahon's Point* (1950)
Oil on canvas 77 × 99·5
Art Gallery of New South Wales

Arthur Boyd b. 1920
Shearers playing for a bride (1957-58)

In the mid-forties, with the financial assistance of his uncle Martin, the novelist, Boyd was able to devote his full time to his art. He made a large mural covering four walls in Martin's home at Berwick, Victoria, and produced a series of tile paintings and ceramic sculptures; during this period successful exhibitions of his work were held in London, Canberra and Geneva.

In 1950 Boyd made a trip to Central Australia which gave rise to the series he painted between 1957 and 1959 on the theme of 'Love, Marriage and the Death of a Half-caste'. About this time he became closely involved with Perceval, Charles Blackman, Clifton Pugh, Robert Dickerson, John Brack and Bernard Smith in the group which called itself the Antipodeans. The group, based in Melbourne, rejected the abstract form which was in vogue in Sydney, claiming instead that the artist's role was as a critic of society.

Since the early sixties Boyd has lived overseas; in 1960 he exhibited at the Zwemmer Gallery in London and the following year he was commissioned to provide the decor for the Renard ballet at the Edinburgh Festival. In 1962 a large retrospective exhibition of his work was held at the Whitechapel Gallery in London. While in London Boyd sought other mediums, and in 1963 a collection of his work sent to the Australian Gallery, Melbourne, contained etchings and drypoints. A recent exhibition, held at Rudy Komon's gallery in Sydney in 1975, marked the publication of a new book, *Arthur Boyd Drawings,* with an introduction by the critic Laurie Thomas.

Boyd's haunting dreams of the half-caste world, wherein the bridegroom's visions of his bride are buried in doubts of himself and fear of the white man, form the series 'Love, Marriage and Death of a Half-caste'. There is an emphasis on the symbol: the moths around the lamp, the lustful ram joining the group of gamblers and the bride. The apprehension on the male faces and the resignation of the bride state bluntly the unease of the theme, as does the contrast between the aboriginal characteristics of the men and the white racial appearance of the bride. The technique used helps the general insistence on the dream world, being explicit in what it says, yet nowhere attempting an illusion of reality.

Represented New South Wales, South Australian, Queensland, Western Australian and (especially) Victorian State galleries; Bendigo gallery; University of Western Australia.

Plate 83 *Shearers playing for a bride* (1957–58)
Oil on canvas 150 × 175·5
National Gallery of Victoria. Presented by Tristan Buesst 1958

Ian Fairweather 1891–1974
Roi soleil (1957)

Fairweather was greatly influenced by Oriental art: perhaps more than any other Australian artist. Long periods he spent in China, Korea, India, and the Pacific Islands gave him a far from superficial knowledge of eastern modes of seeing, and of calligraphic brushwork. Often a resemblance to the American Mark Tobey can be seen, but this is due rather to the similar backgrounds of the artists than to any direct influence.

Most of Fairweather's works are in gouache (water-based paint) on cardboard grounds, since he is allergic to oil paint. The gouache has given a matt surface to his paintings, which, with the predominance of earth colours, makes for a most appropriate softness of effect. The board has been adopted through the difficulty of obtaining materials in many locations.

In *Roi soleil* the 'Sun King' is not Louis XIV, but the linear equivalent of some primitive Eastern deity, gesticulating from his throne through a cubist screen.

Ian Fairweather was born in Scotland in 1891 and spent his boyhood on the island of Jersey. During World War One he was captured in France and spent four years as a prisoner of war in Holland, during which time he did some painting and began studying Chinese calligraphy.

In the ensuing years, Fairweather travelled extensively. He spent one year in Canada and six in China, then travelled through Manila, Davao, Bali and Zamboanga, arriving in Australia in 1934. In Melbourne he became friendly with William Frater, George Bell and Arnold Shore but, although he had a city studio and held an exhibition, his work attracted only modest interest and he subsequently resumed his travels. He served in the Army in India in World War Two and returned to Australia in 1943.

In 1952 Fairweather set out from Darwin in a raft he had built and made a sixteen-day crossing to Timor, where he was detained by Indonesian authorities for three months before being sent to Singapore. He later travelled to England, writing a book on the way about his raft journey. His attempts to get the book published in England, however, were unsuccessful and he was forced to take work digging ditches in Devonshire. Eventually he returned to Australia and settled on Bribie Island, Queensland.

Represented New South Wales, Victorian, South Australian, Queensland, Western Australian and Tasmanian State galleries; Ballarat gallery.

Plate 84 *Roi soleil* (1957)
Gouache on pulpboard 99 × 72·5
Art Gallery of New South Wales

William Dobell 1899–1970

Helena Rubinstein (undated c. 1957)

Dobell painted three major portraits of Helena Rubinstein as well as smaller sketches, all from sittings she gave him when re-visiting Australia in 1957. This, the first major version, shows the sitter as the strong decisive creator of a huge industrial empire. Alert intelligence dominates and the technique matches: swift, bold brushwork states exactly what is to be said. Power is in the tense pose and the watchful expression, no less than in the warm colour scheme accentuated by tiny touches of blue; in the contrasts between dark and light, and in the economy of means. There is at the same time a remoteness, expressed by the enlargement of the arms which tilts the figure back, as though she recoiled from the spectator.

The 1940s saw a new phase in Dobell's career. In 1941 he resigned his teaching post at East Sydney Technical School and went to work for the Allied Works Council, painting camouflage at Bankstown aerodrome and making a series of studies of wartime activities.

Dobell had now gained a considerable reputation. Between 1940 and 1943 four of his paintings, including *Mrs South Kensington*, were purchased by the Art Gallery of New South Wales, and in 1943 twenty-eight of his works appeared in Sydney Ure Smith's *Australian Present-Day Art*.

Though Dobell had entered the Archibald Prize since 1940, he was not successful in the competition until 1943 when he entered *Brian Penton*, *The billy boy* and *Joshua Smith*—any one of which, it has been said, could have won the award. However, when the prize was ultimately awarded to the portrait of Dobell's friend and fellow-painter Joshua Smith, the decision provoked a storm of controversy. This culminated in a court action brought by two of the unsuccessful entrants who claimed that the trustees of the Art Gallery of New South Wales had breached the terms of the prize by awarding it for a work which, it was argued, was a caricature.

Although the action was lost, Dobell was greatly upset by the ensuing publicity; he suffered a nervous breakdown which caused his left leg to be paralysed for a time and for twelve months he stopped painting.

Plate 85 *Helena Rubinstein* (undated *c.* 1957)
Oil on hardboard 98 × 99
National Gallery of Victoria. Felton Bequest 1964

William Dobell 1899–1970
Dame Mary Gilmore (1955-57)

The portrait of Dame Mary Gilmore was commissioned by the Australian Book Society when the poet was ninety years old. She sits alert with her hands before her on the arms of the chair. The pyramid of the blue-green gown is crowned by her tiny head with its provocative expression and wonderful eyes. It is difficult to look at the remainder of the painting once her gaze has captured one's own. The wisdom of the great poet is combined with the wisdom of ninety years, and the whole has become greater than the parts: it may well be Dobell's finest work. We can examine the scumbled colour, the bold symbolic drapery, the linear rhythm if we force ourselves, but the face, small though it is, dominates all. It is not surprising that Dobell took two years to complete the portrait.

When Dobell resumed painting after the 'Joshua Smith' affair, he at first produced only landscapes, many depicting the country around Wangi Wangi, on the shores of Lake Macquarie, twenty-five miles from Newcastle, where he had exiled himself and where he was to live for most of the rest of his life.

In 1949, however, he was awarded both the Archibald and Wynne Prizes, becoming the first painter to win both prizes in the same year. His portrait of Margaret Olley won him the Archibald while the Wynne was awarded for *Storm approaching, Wangi*. The following year he visited New Guinea and produced the first of what was to be a major series of 'New Guinea paintings', later exhibited in 1954. In 1957 his *Helena Rubinstein* won the Women's Weekly portrait prize and in 1960 he won the Archibald prize for the third time with his portrait of Dr Edward MacMahon, the Sydney surgeon who, two years earlier, treated Dobell for cancer. In the same year his portrait of Sir Robert Menzies appeared on the cover of *Time* magazine.

In 1961 Dobell was commissioned by the Duke of Edinburgh to paint two works for the Windsor Castle collection; other works were shown in London at the Whitechapel Gallery and he visited Saigon and Hong Kong for *Time*.

Such was Dobell's reputation that an auction of his paintings in the Norman Schureck collection in 1962 brought the highest prices ever paid for the works of a living Australian artist.

Represented Victorian, South Australian, Queensland, Tasmanian, and (especially) New South Wales and Western Australian State galleries; Bendigo and Ballarat galleries; Australian National War Memorial, Canberra.

Plate 86 *Dame Mary Gilmore* (1955–57)
Oil on masonite 90 × 73·5
Art Gallery of New South Wales. Gift of Dame Mary Gilmore 1960

Robert Dickerson b. 1924

Tired man (undated c. 1957)

Dickerson was twenty-six before he took up painting (he had received no formal training at that time and has had none since) and more than a decade was to pass before he decided to give his full time to painting.

Born in Hurstville, Sydney, in 1924, Dickerson took a keen interest in drawing at State school. He left school when he was fourteen to take a job as a process worker but a year later (under the name of Bobby Moody) he began a brief career as a professional boxer, at first fighting three rounds at the Sydney Stadium for about £2 a bout, then working up to ten rounds. Shortly after the outbreak of the World War Two he enlisted in the RAAF where he spent four years, serving in Darwin and Indonesia. On his discharge he became a professional punter for about twelve months until he realized that this was scarcely a profitable pursuit. He then took a job as a concrete worker. A friend, William Sewell, who was a commercial artist, suggested that Dickerson take up painting; this he did with great zeal, at one stage producing a painting a night while he continued to work during the day. In 1954 he won the Clint Prize and in 1956 held his first one-man exhibition at the Gallery of Contemporary Art; he failed to sell a single canvas, and disillusionment and a bout of pleurisy caused him to stop painting. Within two years, however, he had resumed.

In 1958 he won second place in the Blake Prize for religious art and about this time he decided that he could stand the boredom of 'working for a pay-packet' no longer and devoted his full time to painting. He won awards at the 1965 Easter Show and the *Mirror*-Waratah competition in 1966.

Dickerson's one theme is the lonely individual. No matter what profession or occupation is ascribed to the figure, it is alone. Even when it is joined by a second, they are indifferent to each other; they meet only for the moment. No more background is provided than is absolutely necessary: in the present case, a bench and a green mound.

Dickerson makes a solid symbol dispassionately. There is no involvement, no compassion, no anger. Here is a tired man. He is lonely. The medium is enamel on hardboard: it is rare for Dickerson to use anything else.

Represented New South Wales, Victorian, South Australian, Queensland, Western Australian and Tasmanian State galleries; Ballarat gallery; Australian National University, Canberra.

Plate 87 *Tired man* (undated *c.* 1957)
Synthetic enamel on hardboard 137 × 152·5
National Gallery of Victoria. Purchased 1957

John Brack b. 1920

Nude with two chairs (1957)

The nude with two chairs is not a nude in the fashionable meaning of 'nude'. It is rather a naked figure having much in common with the naked chairs, set, as is usual in Brack's paintings, in a rather bare corner of a world that is far from cluttered. It is Brack's genius that, in this minute piece of all the universe, so much of the truth of the whole is conveyed. We are invited to take a cool objective look at a human being, not one selected to illustrate a point but one who exemplifies the whole species. Every line counts, every one of the shapes and astringent colours belongs. It is an intellectual exercise and yet it relates to all we see and know. This is what the world is like when all irrelevencies have been removed.

John Brack was in his early thirties by the time he was able to devote much time to painting, and almost fifty before he made painting his full-time pursuit.

Born in 1920 he left school to take a job as an insurance clerk, at the same time attending evening classes at the Melbourne gallery school. During World War Two he served with the artillery in the AIF but in 1946 resumed his studies, and for three years was a full-time student at the gallery school under William Dargie. On his graduation he obtained a post as an assistant in the gallery's print room and spent two years in this job before being appointed painting master at Melbourne Grammar School.

Up till this time Brack produced relatively little work, but since his new post was for only two days a week he was now able to spend more time on his own painting. In 1953 his painting *The barber's shop* was exhibited at the Peter Bray Gallery in Melbourne and subsequently purchased by the National Gallery of Victoria; in the same year he held his first one man show at the same gallery and later held other exhibitions in Melbourne, Sydney, Adelaide and Brisbane. During this period Brack was an occasional lecturer at the National Gallery of Victoria and the Fine Arts department of Melbourne University; in 1959 he exhibited with the Antipodean group.

Teaching remained his main employment, however, and in 1963 he was appointed head of the National Gallery's school. He held the post for five years, during which time the school was modernised and its status increased. He resigned in 1968 to devote his full time to painting.

Represented New South Wales, Victorian, South Australian and Western Australian State galleries; Ballarat gallery.

Plate 88 *Nude with two chairs* (1957)
Oil on canvas 81·5×61
Art Gallery of New South Wales

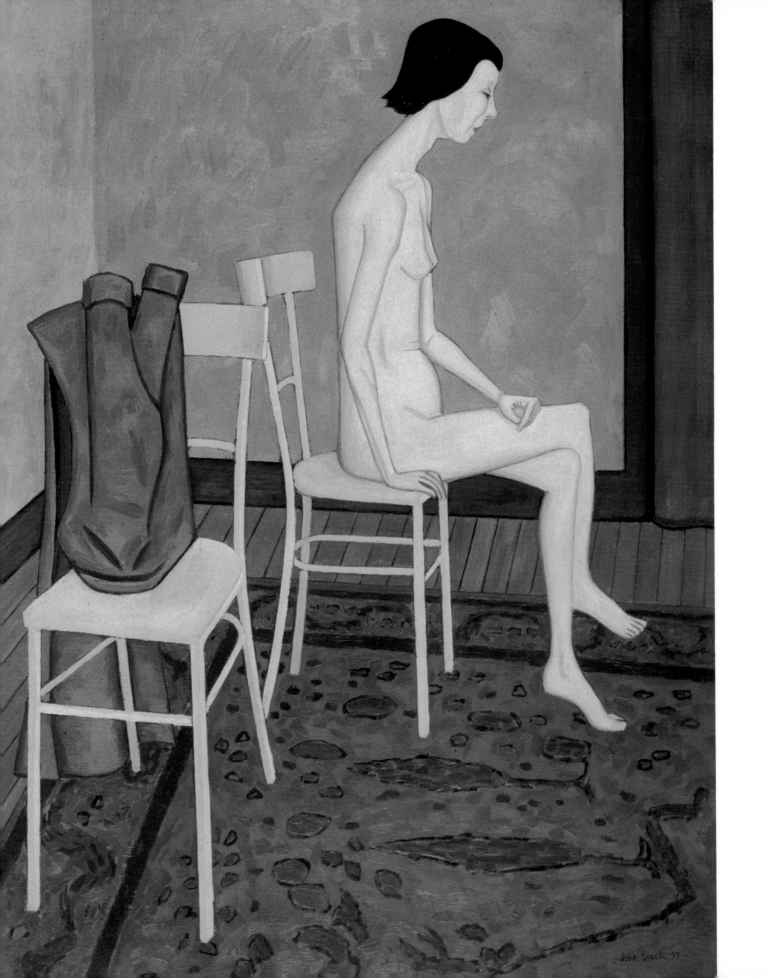

Clifton Pugh b. 1924
The eagle and the Baobab trees (1957)

Pugh's world is the Bush—a world made of stones and trees, grasses and flowers, sometimes drab and sometimes brilliant, and usually inhabited by monsters: dead or living animals, burnt stumps, even people. His work sometimes resembles that of Graham Sutherland or Paul Nash. In the present example a stump rears in the foreground, only slightly less menacing than the eagle behind it. The setting is strange: the contorted rock below echoes the jagged stump and jagged bird, while the baobab could form a design for trees on the moon. Here is a landscape with no love for man, inhabited by creatures who share its dislike. Although the effect is emotional Pugh's years of training in a tonal mode of expression are always evident. He uses tone to create form and pattern.

Pugh's parents were amateur artists but, although he drew well at school, he left without any firm intention to make art his career. As a lad he tried to enlist in the Army at the outbreak of the World War Two but was rejected because he was under age. In 1943 his enlistment was accepted and he subsequently served in New Guinea.

On his discharge in 1947 Pugh began a rehabilitation course at the National Gallery of Victoria's school under William Dargie. His studies continued until the early fifties when he broke with Dargie's teaching and went his own way. At Cottle's Bridge, twenty-five miles from Melbourne, he built a wattle and daub house where he lived with his wife and family and raised poultry.

Pugh is well-known for his portraits and has won the Archibald Prize three times.

Represented New South Wales, Victorian, South Australian, Queensland and Western Australian State galleries; Bendigo, Ballarat and Castlemaine galleries; Australian National University, Canberra; University of Queensland.

Plate 89 *The eagle and the Baobab trees* (1957)
Oil on masonite 66 × 89
Art Gallery of New South Wales

Ray Crooke b. 1922
Mission tank (undated c. 1958)

Ray Crooke is a painter of Northern Australia and the Pacific Islands. He is at home in the tropics and therefore finds the influence of Gauguin almost obligatory. People are important to him—but people within a landscape. Virgin country is rare in his work: as a rule there are at least houses or tents, but more often aborigines, natives, prospectors. In *Mission tank* the people dominate the mission, seen in the distance. Five aborigines are assembled to have their pictures painted. They sit or stand across the foreground to make a coloured pattern, and as one would expect from an admirer of Gauguin, this is the key to Crooke's art. He makes of nature a pattern: the subject of the picture is always colour significantly arranged. The areas of dark and light, blue or brown, are expertly assembled; the lines calculated for their effect. Light and subject matter are only important as they assist this ideal.

Ray Crooke was born at Auburn, Victoria, in 1922, the second of three brothers. His grandmother was a painter of miniatures and his father had studied art at the National Gallery school until family difficulties forced him to abandon his course. His son was luckier; he left High School, took a job in an advertising agency and attended night classes in art at Swinburne Technical College.

Crooke served for four years in the army during World War Two but continued his studies by taking a correspondence course from East Sydney Technical College. On his discharge he again studied, this time as a rehabilitation student, at Swinburne. While still a student he held a show and sold most of the paintings and drawings he had made during the war. A second show was less than successful and he decided to move to Sydney. After a brief stint as a commercial artist he headed for Torres Strait, which had fascinated him during the war, and for a time worked on a lugger as a diver for Trochus shell.

In the late fifties Crooke's paintings of the island and other localities in north Queensland were exhibited at the Australian Gallery in Melbourne. This was followed by another successful exhibition in Brisbane in 1961 and the family moved north again, this time to settle at Yorkey's Knob, near Cairns. His work was included in the 1963 exhibition of Australian art at the Tate Gallery, London, and in 1966 he went to Vietnam on commission as an official war artist.

Represented New South Wales, South Australian, Queensland, Western Australian and Tasmanian State galleries; University of Western Australia.

Plate 90 *Mission tank* (undated *c.* 1958)
Oil on hardboard 100 × 75
Reproduced by courtesy of the owner, State College, Toorak

John Perceval b. 1923
Dairy farm (1960)

John Perceval's landscapes are painted from nature, on the spot; he carries on the *plein-air* tradition of the Heidelberg School. Many influences have made his style but they are not easy to unravel, being all completely assimilated—though an early interest in Van Gogh remains. It is very evident that Perceval is occupied with the visual. Form—Berenson's 'tactile values'—is not important to him, nor is pattern. What matters is the delight in the thing seen and its expression in terms of colour and texture, leaving the trace of the brush as evidence of the excitement generated by the subject itself.

John Perceval was born in 1923 at Bruce Rock, Western Australia, and grew up on his father's farm at Merridin. He began drawing when a small child, encouraged by his mother who was herself an amateur painter. When he was ten his mother took him to live in Perth and two years later, to Melbourne.

Perceval taught himself to paint, copying reproductions of the works of such artists as Van Gogh. In Melbourne he met the artist Arnold Shore who recognized the youth's talent and gave him his first set of oil paints.

In the thirties he worked for a time on a dairy farm, and later as a window-dresser, but with the outbreak of World War Two joined the Army. Here, while working in the cartographic section of the Army Survey Corps he met Arthur Boyd and became friendly with Albert Tucker and Sidney Nolan. After the war he married Boyd's sister Mary and they lived at the Boyd family pottery in Murrumbeena. For some months during 1949 he also studied at the Melbourne gallery school.

In the early forties he had exhibited with the Contemporary Art Society and a few years later made a series of paintings with religious themes, but increasingly pottery became his main occupation. In 1958 he exhibited the series of ceramic 'angels' which were to become the best-known examples of his work in this medium.

Perceval went to London in 1962 and spent three years there before returning to Australia to take up a fellowship at the Australian National University.

Represented New South Wales, Victorian, South Australian and Queensland State galleries; Launceston gallery; Melbourne University, Monash University, University of Western Australia and Australian National University, Canberra.

Plate 91 *Dairy farm* (1960)
Oil on canvas 91·5 × 113·5, mounted on masonite
Art Gallery of New South Wales

Charles Blackman b. 1928

Dreaming in the street (1960)

Blackman's world is inhabited by quiet figures, solitary even in groups, withdrawn into themselves in a void: there is rarely a background and only the slightest suggestion of properties. In *Dreaming in the street* what at first appear to be shadows on a rear wall prove to be additional figures; the ground is not included, a flower is merely a red shape, and none of this matters. We are content with the figures: faces half hidden, eyes averted. They live their inner lives in dream worlds, hinted at but not explained. When Blackman departs from his private theme it is to explore the dream-worlds of others, for example the 'Alice in Wonderland' or the 'Sleeping Beauty' series. Even his boats have the quality of faerie barges.

The mood is one of compassion. The mystery and the drama of light in no way inspire dread. While the spectator is not invited into the picture his sympathy is aroused: it is the antithesis of abstract art yet its pictorial qualities are in many ways the same.

Charles Blackman was born in Sydney in 1928 but spent his early years in Queensland. His father, who died when Blackman was still a child, had artistic talent and his stepfather was a house-painter and decorator. Blackman's own talent for drawing led his mother to get him a job at the age of fourteen as a copy boy and press artist on the *World's News*; he later enrolled in night classes at East Sydney Technical School and in 1945 began working as a press artist on the Sydney *Sun*.

Blackman left newspaper work to hitchhike at leisure along the east coast between Brisbane and Melbourne. In Brisbane he met and married Barbara Patterson and in 1952 the couple settled in Melbourne.

After a short trip back to Queensland in 1955 Blackman met the gallery owner Georges Mora and in 1957 exhibited his 'Alice in Wonderland' series.

Blackman was one of the seven artists who contributed to the Antipodean Exhibition of 1959; in 1960 he won the Crouch Prize and the same year *Dreaming in the street* helped him to win the Helena Rubinstein Travelling Scholarship. Following these successes he went to London and Europe. He exhibited at the Whitechapel and Tate galleries in London and was one of three Australians whose work was included in the 1961 Paris Biennale.

Represented New South Wales, Victorian, South Australian, Queensland and Western Australian State galleries; Ballarat gallery; University of Western Australia.

Plate 92 *Dreaming in the street* (1960)
Oil on board 122 × 183
National Gallery of Victoria. Purchased 1960

Lawrence Daws b. 1927

Sungazer III (1961)

On a first casual inspection this large and decorative canvas appears to be an abstraction. Then the sungazer resolves himself, standing on the right, ill-defined as though he stood for all men or any man. His legs suggest the aborigine, his head an automaton or a mask. The red landscape might be Australian hills, the sun might be setting for the day or dying for all eternity. The pervading red is inimical: we are so certainly in a landscape in which only the sungazer lives, in which nothing else could stay alive.

The painting makes a fundamental statement about the Australian outback, where only the sun lives in its own right and all other life is there only on sufferance.

Lawrence Daws was born in Adelaide in 1927 and spent two years studying architecture and geology in Adelaide before going to New Guinea, when he was twenty, to work with an oil exploration company. On his return to Australia in 1950 he enrolled at the Melbourne gallery school and studied there under William Dargie for three years. For two years after that he travelled in the outback, painting and exploring for minerals, then spent a year teaching at St Peter's College in Adelaide.

In 1956 Daws was awarded the Flotto-Lauro-Dante Alighieri Scholarship in art which enabled him to spend two years studying in Rome; his first important one-man show was subsequently held there at the La Salita gallery. In 1960 he returned to Australia for six months but since that time he has been living in London, although he has made several visits to Australia.

Daws has travelled widely in Europe and America, and in 1961 his work, with that of Brett Whitely and Charles Blackman, formed the Australian representation at the Paris Biennale. He also exhibited at the Tate Gallery, London, the following year and was represented at the Sao Paulo Biennale in Brazil. In 1962 he held a one-man show at the Matthieson Gallery, London.

A retrospective exhibition of Daws' work was organized to coincide with the 1966 Adelaide Festival of Arts.

Represented New South Wales, Victorian, Queensland, Western Australian, Tasmanian and (especially) South Australian State galleries; Ballarat and Mildura galleries; University of Western Australia.

Plate 93 *Sungazer III* (1961)
Oil on canvas 173 × 167
National Gallery of Victoria. A. R. Henderson Bequest 1963

Russell Drysdale b. 1912
Mangula (1961)

In recent years Drysdale's interest has turned more and more to the aboriginal inhabitants of those landscapes which once he presented as empty or containing one or two lonely whites. These newer paintings began with his visit to Cape York, the most northerly tip of Australia, in 1951. At first the familiar landscapes were peopled by appropriately clad or unclad figures, perhaps more realistically painted than the setting behind them. Latterly these figures have often been set into a background which no longer appears as a landscape, but as rocks or, as in *Mangula,* the grave posts of Melville Island. The colours are still reds, browns, and yellows, but less is made of their relationship with reality. The canvas has become a pattern of angular and rounded forms: it is almost a step towards abstraction. The size has become larger too, so that intimacy has given way to grandeur.

In October, 1960, a retrospective exhibition of Drysdale's works was held at the Art Gallery of New South Wales (an honour rarely accorded a living artist). The show contained 108 of Drysdale's works and followed closely on a successful exhibition at the Leicester Galleries in London. In 1962 Drysdale was appointed to the Commonwealth Art Advisory Board (a post which he held until his resignation in 1973) and the following year he was made a trustee of the Art Gallery of New South Wales.

A definitive monograph of Drysdale's works by the author and critic Geoffrey Dutton was published by Thames and Hudson in 1964, and in the same year a further retrospective exhibition was held at the John Martin Galleries, Adelaide, to coincide with the Adelaide Festival of Arts. In 1965, Drysdale was awarded a Britannica Australia Award for his contribution to the arts. He was knighted in 1969.

Represented Victorian, South Australian, Queensland, Western Australian, Tasmanian and (especially) New South Wales State galleries; Geelong, Newcastle and Ballarat galleries.

Plate 94 *Mangula* (1961)
Oil on canvas 183 × 122
Art Gallery of New South Wales. Florence Turner Blake Bequest Fund

John Olsen b. 1928

Journey into You Beaut Country No. 1 (1961)

Olsen's approach is through the emotions, particularly emotions uninhibited by conscious thought. His intention is to get onto his canvas the whole feeling of a place or occassion, not a part only, and to do this execution must be rapid. That his pictures have great decorative qualities is incidental. There is an affinity with child art which naturally occurs, since children too seek an expression of their emotions about the subject of their pictures. However, theirs is an innocent expression, while Olsen has behind him skills and knowledge beyond the resources of a child. His problem is to avoid allowing this skill and knowledge to intrude so as to dull or even nullify the impact of his original idea.

As *Journey into You Beaut Country No. 1* is examined, birds and animals appear among tree forms.

John Olsen was born at Newcastle in 1928 but when he was seven his family moved to Sydney where his father was a salesman. After his schooling at Paddington Junior Technical School and St Joseph's College, Hunters Hill, Olsen got a job as a junior clerk in a shipping office. His ambition at this time was to become a newspaper cartoonist and he enrolled in night classes at Julian Ashton's, under John Passmore, in the hope of improving his drawing. He also studied with the painter Desiderius Orban.

Olsen had his first show in 1952 and its results were encouraging. His first significant success, however, came in 1955, when one of his paintings was bought by the National Gallery of Victoria from the Melbourne *Herald* outdoor art show. Up to this time his work had followed the academic tradition but by 1956 he had turned to Abstract Impressionism, and together with Klippel, Rose, Passmore and Smith he contributed to the exclusively abstract exhibition, Directions I.

In the same year a Sydney critic organized a scheme to send Olsen abroad for three years. He studied engraving under Heyter in Paris and painted on the island of Majorca where he became friendly with the poet Robert Graves.

In 1963 Olsen began designing a series of tapestries to be made in Portugal and later went to Europe to further his work in this medium, remaining abroad until 1967. He recently completed a large (70 feet by ten feet) mural, commissioned at a cost of $35,000 by the Dobell Foundation, for the Sydney Opera House.

Represented New South Wales, Victorian, Queensland, Western Australian and Tasmanian State galleries; Newcastle gallery.

Plate 95 *Journey into You Beaut Country No. 1* (1961)
Oil on hardboard 152 × 102
National Gallery of Victoria. Purchased 1961

Leonard French b. 1928
Death and transfiguration (1961)

The most obvious and appealing quality of French's paintings is decoration. Great glowing forms shine brightly from rich dark grounds, or glow dimly through layer upon layer of glaze. They abound with symbols, some personal, some universal, and are far from being the purely decorative arrangements they first appear.

In *Death and transfiguration* the picture is divided into two. On a lower level are the dead, in form between a fish—an ancient symbol for the Christian—and a human body. Each is enclosed in his own coffin-like compartment. Above, in glittering triumph, is the resurrected martyr, not only resurrected but transfigured.

Leonard French made his first paintings when he was eleven, using a spot in a disused pottery as a 'studio' and made his first mural (for a local church) when he was nineteen.

After leaving school in the Melbourne suburb of Brunswick where he was born, his father got him a job with a local plumber but he later completed a five-year apprenticeship with a sign-writer.

French abandoned sign-writing the day his apprenticeship ended, determined to make painting his life. In 1949, when he was twenty-one, he held his first one-man exhibition at a Melbourne gallery; it was not only praised by the critics but brought him £160 from sales. Following the exhibition he worked his way to Europe where he spent eighteen months (mostly in Ireland).

On his return to Melbourne in 1951 French worked for a time as a sign-writer, then as a teacher in the Victorian Education Department. The first of his 'Iliad' series was exhibited the following year and in 1955 the larger 'Odyssey' series was shown at the Victorian Artists' Society.

French's painting was influenced at first by Eastern and later Byzantine art, a phase which reached its culmination in his 1962 series of mural-sized paintings based on the life of the sixteenth century martyr Edmund Campion. In that year French went to Greece to further his study of Byzantine art, returning in 1963 to begin a commission for the ninety-foot-long stained glass ceiling for the Great Hall of the Victorian Arts Centre. He went to Japan and America in 1965 and supervised the completion of the ceiling in 1967.

Represented New South Wales, Victorian, Queensland, Western Australian and Tasmanian State galleries; Ballarat gallery; University of Western Australia.

Plate 96 *Death and transfiguration* (1961)
Enamel, collage and gold leaf on hessian on hardboard 122 × 138
Art Gallery of New South Wales. Sir Charles Lloyd Jones Bequest Fund 1962

Jeffrey Smart b. 1921

Cahill Expressway (1962)

Here is the heart of Sydney, but it might be anywhere. Smart is not concerned with the 'typical' Australian landscape nor with the romantic past. His subjects are very much of the present, with an eye on the future. Unlike most of his predecessors he forsakes the 'long ago and far away'. He paints reality—stark reality—and by its very starkness makes his a magic world. It is very much a world made by Man. Grass sometimes appears between stones, and trees are very rarely seen, but what fascinates Smart is the strange form created by human endeavour. His work could be regarded as a tribute to technology, existing for its own sake, for few people inhabit these roads and buildings, all of them public places. Yet it is something beyond that: its passionate detail forces us to reflect on its existence, and our own.

Jeffrey Smart was born in Adelaide in 1921 and studied at the South Australian School of Arts and Crafts. He later taught art for the South Australian Education Department and at the King's School, Sydney, and East Sydney Technical School.

In 1949 and 1950 Smart studied in Paris under Fernand Leger at the Académie Montmartre and at La Grande Chaumière. On his return to Australia he won the Commonwealth Jubilee Open Art Competition in 1951, and in 1954–55 was art critic for the *Daily Telegraph*.

Three of Smart's works were included in the 1962 exhibition of Australian art held at the Tate Gallery, London, and after painting for several years in Italy he held an exhibition at the Redfern Gallery, London, in 1967. He now lives in Italy.

Represented New South Wales, Victorian, South Australian and Western Australian State galleries; Newcastle gallery.

Plate 97 *Cahill Expressway* (1962)
Oil on plywood 81 × 111·5
National Gallery of Victoria. Purchased 1963

Arnold Shore 1897–1963
Bushscape, Clonbinane (1962)

Like a number of his contemporaries, Shore's first contact with art was as a designer of stained glass, and the preoccupation with colour remained with him all his life. Fascinated by the Australian bush and extremely sensitive to its form, colour and texture, he forms a link joining McCubbin and Williams. He has, however, considerable qualities of his own. He captures what the nineteenth century was fond of calling 'The Spirit of the Bush', but, unlike the early McCubbin, he did not see it as hostile or indifferent. It is a friendly, beautiful, even enchanted world, which invites the spectator to enter. Shore was able to bring to the bushland an excitement in the presence of nature that had not been seen in Australian landscape painting since the waning of the Heidelberg School.

Arnold Shore was born at Windsor, Melbourne, in 1897, the seventh child of a coach-maker. After leaving Prahran West State School at the age of twelve he worked for six years—from 1911 to 1917—with the Melbourne glass merchants Brooks Robinson, first as a messenger, then as a designer of stained glass in the company's studios. For five years he studied part-time at the Melbourne gallery school under Frederick McCubbin and L. Bernard Hall, then left to become a student of Max Meldrum who had recently returned from Paris.

For a time Shore was strongly influenced by Meldrum's theories but in the early twenties he broke with Meldrum's teachings and went his own way.

Shore sent work to the Royal Academy in London and the Autumn Salon in Paris but he also became prominent as a pioneer teacher of post-impressionism in Australia. In company with George Bell he established the first school of modern art in Melbourne in 1932 and in the same year exhibited at the first Melbourne show of the Sydney-based Contemporary Group. When Bell went overseas for more than a year Shore ran the school in his absence and also deputised for Bell as art critic of the Melbourne *Sun*. He shared first prize in the Melbourne *Herald*'s Picture of the Year contest in 1937 (with John Longstaff), won the Crouch Prize in 1938 and the McPhillimy Prize (Geelong) in 1939;

For the greater part of his adult life Shore was a professional critic and lecturer on art. He was art critic for the *Argus* from 1951 to 1956 and for the *Age* from 1957 to 1963.

Represented New South Wales, Victorian, South Australian, Queensland and Western Australian State galleries; Bendigo, Ballarat and Castlemaine galleries.

Plate 98 *Bushscape, Clonbinane* (1962)
Oil on canvas 68·5 × 50
Reproduced by courtesy of the owner, Mrs Arnold Shore

Fred Williams b. 1927

Trees on hillside II (1964)

It might be thought that after hundreds of painters had worked over the Australian landscape for a hundred years their thousands of paintings would cover every aspect of that subject. It has been the remarkable achievement of Fred Williams to find and express a hitherto neglected facet of Australia: the evocative patterns of gumtrees, aligned in forests or distributed thinly among rocks and grasslands.

The first impression is of crudely applied paint on a dull-coloured background, but anyone who has experienced inland Australia will receive immediately the sensations of the hot dry earth, the trees so determinedly un-green, their shapes so unlike the symmetrical compact descendants of European vegetation. The bush, which we tend to think of as though it was all one, has in fact a different prospect for each observer. Using a thoroughly twentieth century idiom, Williams has revealed a mood and a world that had, before him, remained unseen and unsuspected.

Fred Williams was born at Richmond, Melbourne, in 1927. Between 1944 and 1949 he studied at the Melbourne gallery school and, during the same period, with the teacher George Bell. In 1951, in company with Ian Armstrong and Harry Rosengrave, he exhibited in Melbourne; later that year he went to London where he studied graphic techniques at the Chelsea School of Arts and the Central School of Arts and Crafts. Here he produced a series of etchings on the theme of English music halls and others of genre and animal studies.

Williams has produced a large number of etchings, linocuts, monotypes and aquatints (he made more than 8,000 in an eight-year period) but since the fifties he has become better-known for his landscapes in oils. His work has been shown internationally at many exhibitions, including those at the Whitechapel Gallery, London in 1961, South-East Asia in 1962, and the Tate Gallery and in Canada in 1963. In the latter year, Williams made his second overseas trip after winning the Helena Rubinstein Travelling Scholarship. His work was shown in Europe in 1964 and 1965 and in Japan in 1965. In 1966 he won the Georges Invitation Prize and the Wynne Prize.

Represented New South Wales, Victorian and Tasmanian State galleries; Newcastle, Ballarat, Mildura, Castlemaine and Launceston galleries; University of Western Australia.

Plate 99 *Trees on hillside II* (1964)
Oil on tempera on hardboard 91·5×122
Art Gallery of New South Wales. Purchased 1965

Albert Tucker b. 1914

Tree (1965)

Albert Tucker is a maker and manipulator of symbols, but *Tree* is apparently a purely realistic painting of a piece of the Australian bush. A few feet of the trunk of a giant eucalyptus rises through the undergrowth among other lesser trees and saplings. All the beauty and subtlety of the bush is present: its colour, texture and form. But as the painting is examined doubts begin to intrude. Is symbolism present after all? Does the great rugged central form represent only a gum tree, or is the strength and impassivity of the forest implied? Do the strange gum blisters—which actually protude from the canvas and are therefore far more conspicuous than they appear in a reproduction—stand for evil forces silently proliferating from within?

Albert Tucker was born at Yarraville, Melbourne, in 1914, the son of a railway worker.

In the depression years he managed to support himself as a freelance illustrator and writer and between 1939 and 1945 exhibited with the Contemporary Art Society. He served in the Army during World War Two and in 1947 spent four months in Japan as an official artist with the Allied occupation forces. On his return later that year he managed to scrape together a little money and set off for Europe where he was to spend the next eleven years travelling and painting. After working in London, Paris and Western Germany, he exhibited in Amsterdam in 1951 and in Paris, with limited success, the following year.

The next three years were spent in Italy. Here he met Sidney Nolan and in 1953 held a joint exhibition with Nolan in Rome. Three of Tucker's paintings were shown in the 1956 Rome Biennale and by the time he returned to London later that year he was establishing a modest reputation. In London Tucker held a one-man show and exhibited in several other shows but the turning point in his career came in 1957 with the purchase of *Lunar landscape* by the Museum of Modern Art in New York.

Tucker went to New York in 1960 and held another one-man show. In the same year he was awarded the first £1,000 Kurt Geiger Endowment, administered by the Melbourne Museum of Modern Art, and returned to Australia.

Represented New South Wales, Victorian, South Australian, Queensland, Western Australian and Tasmanian State galleries; Bendigo and Newcastle galleries; National Collection, Canberra.

Plate 100 *Tree* (1965)
Acrylic on hardboard 121·5 × 152
National Collection, Canberra

Index

Produced by
John Currey, O'Neil Pty Ltd for
RIGBY LIMITED
Adelaide Sydney Melbourne Brisbane Perth
First published 1973
Reprinted, with revisions, 1975
Third printing 1976
Fourth printing, with revisions, 1977
© John Currey, O'Neil Pty Ltd
National Library of Australia Registry Card Number
and ISBN 0 85179 514 5
Designed by John Sayers
Text set in Monotype Garamond by
Dudley E. King, Melbourne
Printed in Hong Kong

All the paintings in this book have been
reproduced with the permission of the owners,
whose assistance at all stages of production
is gratefully acknowledged.